The Glow Upon The Fringe

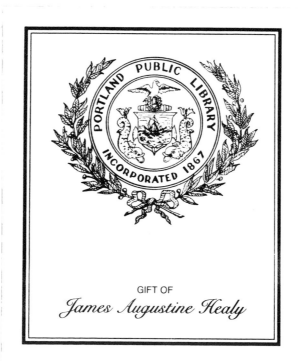

I know the voice of this eloquent river: it talks to me, and to the woods and the rocks, in the same tongue and dialect wherein the Roe discoursed to me as a child; in its crystalline gush my heart and brain are bathed; and I hear, in its plaintive chime, all the blended voices of history, of prophecy, and poesy, from the beginning. I delight in poets who delight in rivers.

John Mitchel
(1815-1875)

Nurchasey to me was paradise. The view from it of Fardness Glen, so beautifully wooded, and of Fardness grazing fields, so green and extensive, together with the effect of these small circular groves, peculiar to some portions of the north, absolutely enchanted me. Nothing, in fact, could surpass my happiness. I frequently dreamt of the scenery about me, although I had it before my eyes every day of the week.

William Carleton
(1794-1869)

The Glow Upon The Fringe

Literary Journeys Around Derry
And The North West

Edited by

SAM BURNSIDE

With an introduction by D.E.S. Maxwell

A Verbal Arts Centre Publication

First published in 1994 by

The Verbal Arts Centre
London Street
Londonderry BT48 6RQ

ISBN 1 898701 05 9

Contents

Acknowledgements

During the creation of this book I received substantial, and always courteous, help from the staff of the Western Education and Library Board's Library Service. Particular thanks go to staff members at Central Library, Londonderry, Library Headquarters, Omagh and Divisional Library, Enniskillen.

For providing photographs, and for permission to use photographs, thanks are due to: The National Library of Ireland, The Arts Council of Northern Ireland, The Western Education and Library Board's Library Service (Irish and Local Studies Department and Media Resources Department), Colm Henry and *Hot Press* for the photograph of Frank McGuinness, Pegeen O'Sullivan for the photograph of her daughter, Margaret Barrington, Lady Elizabeth Macrory for the photograph of her husband, Patrick Macrory, Rachel Brown for the photograph of Cathal Ó Searcaigh, *Field Day Theatre Company* for the photograph of the Field Day directors, Nora Harkin and Bill Webster for the photograph of Peadar O'Donnell, Lesley Doyle for the photograph of Robin Glendinning, Derry City Council for permission to use a detail from the Scriveners' window in the Guildhall. And, among others, Seamus Heaney, Jennifer Johnston, James Simmons, Séamas MacAnnaidh, Robert Greacen, John Kelly, Frank Ormsby, Kathleen Ferguson and Anne Dunlop for supplying photographs and giving permission to use photographs.

Thanks for permission to quote from published works is due to: Faber and Faber Limited, Lapwing Publications, John Kelly/Blackstaff, Frank Ormsby/Gallery Press and Matthew Sweeney. While every attempt has been made to contact all copyright holders, the Verbal Arts Centre apologises for any errors or omissions in the above list, and would be happy to be notified of any corrections to be incorporated in a future edition.

An undertaking such as this is very much a cooperative venture and I wish to thank all those who helped in any way, including Joe Mc Allister for typesetting, Aislinn Duffield for advice and for keeping many technical pieces together so efficiently, Darren James for his work on the photographs, Ralph Dobson for illustrations and cover design, Anne Craig for advice on Irish language matters, Anne McCartney and Annesley Malley for drawing my attention to things I had overlooked and to Sean McMahon for his textual advice. Finally, thanks to all members of the Verbal Arts Centre team for their constant support.

The Verbal Arts Centre is pleased to acknowledge the financial assistance of the following bodies: the Arts Council of Northern Ireland, Derry City Council, Fermanagh District Council, Limavady District Council, Omagh District Council, Strabane District Council and the Ulster Local History Trust.

Finally, my thanks to Bridget O'Toole, Cahal Dallat, Diarmaid Ó Doibhlin and Marion Ross for their cooperation, their contributions and their courtesy, and to D.E.S. Maxwell for his introduction.

Introduction

D.E.S. Maxwell

My memories of growing up in Derry in the nineteen thirties and forties are on the whole affectionate. What Hugh in *Translations* calls the *'desiderium nostrorum* – the need for our own', is a commendable feeling, provided it stays this side of Gloccamorratry. My sentiment harbours a certain wariness. Brian Friel has spoken of Derry as 'gentle, sleepy', but also 'frustrated and frustrating'. Seamus Deane's 'Derry', quoted by Bridget O'Toole, pungently identifies 'the unemployment in our bones'. The poem speaks to the frustrations of a city which was a political vacuum, its Catholic majority virtually disenfranchised by a contemptuous and unrepresentative administration. The affection must acknowledge the brutalities.

There were dissident voices, in unlikely places: Tom Finnegan of Magee College; an Englishman, a Mr Halliday who ran, I think, a cramming school. Though their mildly left-wing activities were disregarded and ineffective, they hark back to the honourable tradition of radicalism described by Cahal Dallat: John Dunlap, Francis Allison, James Porter, Peadar O'Donnell; the generally apolitical nosethumbing of James Simmons is refreshingly subversive too.

Such a roll-call does much to nourish the affection, and this book amply demonstrates the almost magical power, in Irish writing, of registering names in imaginative acts of placement. So as Bridget O'Toole reminds us, Charles Macklin's O'Dougherty sets his 'fine sounding Milesian names' against the pallid 'your Jones and your Homes, your Rice and your Price, your Heads and your Foots'.

Above all, place names inspire the process of, as Sam Burnside puts it, 'identifying self and other'. I think of Seamus Heaney's 'The tawny guttural water / spells itself: Moyola'. Frank Harvey's recital in *Faith Healer* of all those dying Welsh villages is not just an itinerary. It is an incantation, appropriate to the miracles he professes; to his own tragedy; and to 'the whole world' of loss and longing. Perfectly set at the end of Frank McGuinness's *Carthaginians*, and picking up on the earlier remembrance of the thirteen dead, the Derry street names, commonplace enough in themselves, take on a sombre dignity: 'What's the world? Shipquay Street and Ferryquay Street and Rossville Street and William Street and the Strand and Great James Street. While I walk the earth, I walk through you, the streets of Derry. If I meet one who knows you and they ask…"How's Derry?" "Surviving, surviving".'

The essays collected here make plain these features of Irish writing as the varied authors of the North West (broadly considered) exemplify them. It is rich territory, local and yet expansive. For Irish writers in English the inheritance of English Literature is inevitably a dominant but not at all the only presence. Seamus Heaney has translated Dante and is attentive to East

European writers. Brian Friel has given us distinctively 'localised' versions of Chekhov and Turgenev. Gaelic still exercises its challenge to find an imaginative English equivalence: Flann O'Brien's *At Swim-Two-Birds*, Heaney's *Sweeney Astray*. And it is lodged in the unmistakably indigenous rhythms and idiom of the English spoken and written here.

The Irish rendering of English transforms an enforcement into an acquisition, an autonomous and vital strain in the English-speaking tradition. Macklin and George Farquhar adopted the mode of English comedy, giving it an Hibernian inflection, and the contribution has continued from Synge to Beckett (whose unsettling landscapes, like those of Flann O'Brien, would be at home in the Tyrone both men knew). Much of the history of this linguistic cohabitation can be traced in these pages, from the pioneering work, described by Marion Ross, of George Sigerson in the nineteenth century, to the revivalist energies of the four Donegal Gaeltacht regions characterised by Diarmaid Ó Doibhlin, not only animating the language but recording a way of life.

Celebrated names congregate in these pages: natives of the scene, incomers, passers-by (Thackeray, Sam Burnside tells us, remarked of Derry's lunatic asylum that it was 'a model of neatness and comfort'). With those already mentioned we meet Joyce Cary, Jennifer Johnston, John Montague, Frank Ormsby, Walter Hegarty, Nell McCafferty; and a host of figures from the past – historians, theologians, poets. It is a virtue of this book that it enlists people whom fashion has, at least for the time, obscured, including an impressive gallery of women writers, among them Kathleen Coyle, Frances Molloy, Anne Crone, Anne Dunlop. And echoing alongside the writer's names are always those of the places which they commune: Derry, the Grianan of Aileach, Dungiven, Ballymagorry, Holyhill, Greencastle, Carndonagh, Glenties…

It is gratifying to find Yeats putting in an appearance. He turns up, with fitting eccentricity, 'on the Enniskillen bus' in the poem by John Kelly which Marion Ross quotes. Yeats was not a great one for the North. Somewhere he speaks with approval about the enthusiastic reception of a Gaelic play in Letterkenny. He included that in the evidence he was making up for a surge of Irish interest in theatre. This he took to be a harbinger of large audiences for his own plays. But this was not to be and Yeats later lamented that the style of drama developed and popularised by the Abbey 'has been to me a discouragement and a defeat'.

That is by the way but not altogether by the way. For all – maybe because of – his vagaries, Yeats is the dominant, indeed domineering, shaper of modern Irish writing. The writers who frequent these pages and, more literally, frequent the locations so vividly evoked in the five journeys, are in a line of succession. Yeats eloquently articulated it, incorporating his unifying sense of both his Gaelic and his Anglo-Irish predecessors. His subject was Ireland, not as disembodied, simplifying emblem, but as scene, people, story, event. 'We are happy,' he wrote, 'when for everything inside us there is an equivalent something outside us.' These recognitions are the source of his generative powers. Very often his poems reach from a district, a scene, a landmark, to the core of feeling and idea. And it is precisely such correspondences which we see emerging in the writers of the North West. Their reflective gaze is turned, as was Yeats's upon views that are idyllic, picturesque, but which may also be bleak and forbidding, like the human passions which are the writer's terrain.

A Literary Map of the North West is an encouragement to re-acquaintance with the region's writers. It might tempt us as well to explore the paths so instructively taken by its authors.

I

Within and Without the Magic Circle

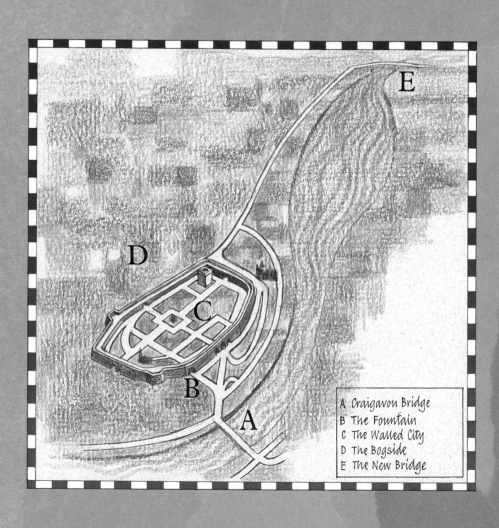

A Craigavon Bridge
B The Fountain
C The Walled City
D The Bogside
E The New Bridge

Within and Without the Magic Circle:
The Literary Heritages of Derry City

Sam Burnside

Sam Burnside's journey leads him through the ancient walled city and out along the urbanised banks of the Foyle. His journey becomes an exploration of the ways in which place and landscape can act upon the imagination, and of how a city's writers can energetically manifest and give expression to its identity through the chemistry of community, landscape and language. As he proceeds, he uncovers a body of creative work that provides evidence of a continuing imaginative enterprise that springs from and throws light on various cultures and traditions, that spans many generations and that makes use of a range of literary forms.

As you cross the Foyle, travelling from the east to the west banks of the river, one of the first things you see is a piece of sculpture raised up at the end of Craigavon Bridge – two figures, standing apart, aloft on rising stone ramparts, with outstretched hands striving to touch, but not quite succeeding, yet. It seems to me that this acknowledges, in a very direct way, the reality of the divisions, and of the distinctions of identities, that exists in Derry, as they do in every place. Yet, within its gesture of outreach the seed of a real hope, and the embodiment of an optimistic aspiration, stand expressed. Here that abstract message is embodied in a piece of public art; but it is as if the place's spirit, and by extension, the spirit of its people, is being given expression. In it there is both welcome to the stranger and reassurance to the citizen.

I have lived in Derry now for a decade and a half; from the beginning, the place intrigued my imagination, just as (for so I gradually came to learn) it has intrigued the minds and imaginations of many others. And as I began to learn about the city and its past, so I grew to know something of the community that exists here and something of its history. Despite its diversity of cultural forms and historical influences, I do not think it possible for anyone associated with the city to describe it, in the accepted and extreme sense of the term, as a divided place, or its people as comprising a divided community; for, while divisions exist (whether social, cultural, religious, sexual, political or class-based), there is something here that subsumes these and relegates them to a place of secondary importance. Firstly, this has to do with the nature of the society, which has grown up in a close, entangled and complex way and is one where everyone is, or claims to be, related to everyone else, so that class, religion and political distinctions never quite reach the purity of absolute demarcation they may assume elsewhere. Secondly, it has to do with a certain magic associated with the physical place and with this (ancient) place's power to have an influence on human experience, and above all on the creative and imaginative life.

This is not altogether a romantic's view. Derry's special appeal was felt by the (typically energetic and pragmatic Victorian) amateur botanist and geologist Robert Lloyd Praeger. The scientist in him recognised and responded to the fact that Derry is in reality an island city, rising up between the Foyle and an ancient body of water that filled the low ground to the north west, and that extended at one time from the Swilly to the Foyle. But the other Praeger, the romantic courser of Ireland's back ways and byways, recognised in this water enclosed piece of land something unique. He identified this in his book *The Way That I Went* (1937) as, 'the magic circle of [Derry's] virginity'. It is this image of the completed circle (the enclosing water, the stone-walled city) and of the spell that is there contained, that indicates the potential for harmony, and of completeness. Columcille felt something of this also, though he (or, more likely, the anonymous medieval poet who interpreted his feelings) articulated it differently:

> Crowded full of heaven's angels
> Is every leaf of the oaks of Derry.

Examples of such responses as these to the place of Derry can be multiplied; when Sean O'Faolain visited the north west he was struck by the almost expressive manner in which history clings to the physical body of the city, and through that to its people. It was from this sense of the place that he considered the city an ideal setting for a novel:

> What I [mean] by this is the atmosphere of [this place] –
> indefinable, impalpable – [it clusters] life into articulate and
> significant relationships. Perhaps it is the atmosphere of his-
> tory; or that the people have adopted a certain kind of
> position, almost a pose, appropriate to the dramatic mean-
> ing of their own kind of life; and this has gone into the very
> stoncs of the town, all its ways and outer signs, as the face
> and body of a man reveals his inner nature.

Leaving Craigavon Bridge behind, to enter the city we proceed up Carlisle Road. Close by is the site of the Opera House. This was a centre for a variety of cultural activities; it was here, for example, that Oscar Wilde came to give two lectures, one on Thursday 3rd and the other on Friday 4th January, 1884 – the first on decorative art and the other an account of his experiences of travelling in America and Canada.

Turning left up Hawkin Street, and passing the grim facade of what was the Women's Penitentiary, the first entrance to the walled city that we find is by New Gate. Using the stone steps leading off Artillery Street one may climb and stand on Derry's walls at this point. From here the eye can follow the curve of the Foyle as it dreams its way down the valley between tree-topped hills. Here you become conscious of how the walled city rests naturally in the crook of the river's cradling arm, and of the dense and nurturing greenery, much of it still comprised of old oak, that husbands the privacy of the surrounding hillsides.

Derry; Daire Calgach; Derry; Doire Colmcille (or Cholmcille); Londonderry; Derry – the names, taken in unison, provide a hymn to the place and a tune to the hopscotch of a dance taken by its tangling history. And, in their origin and variety, the names provide a clue to the enduring significance of language, of its intimate links to the true nature of those who use it, of the peculiarly pragmatic yet mythic nature of history itself when it is seen as a tangible, tactile thing. Through the medium of language, history leaves its taste-imprint on the tongues of succeeding generations – and, perhaps most importantly for the inhabitants of a city that had long awareness of the nature of borders and boundaries, the significance of the act of naming, of identifying self and other and of the absolute centrality of language in its defining (and thus lawgiving) function.

On the streets surrounding us, in the pubs, in the workplaces, talk abounds and here is as great indeed as it is reputed to be in Dublin; conversation is peppered with wit, but sharpened too by an instinct for brevity. This is fuelled by many ellipses based on the shared meanings and on the instinctive understandings that only a close community can harbour. This is something that only a community strong in its own rootedness can continue to nurture in an age when storytelling and tongue entertainment is, it seems, a thing, almost everywhere, of the past. Although this is an oral tradition something of the community warmth that is associated with it is contained both in the title and the content of Tomás O Canáinn's *Home to Derry* (1986).

The talk is full too of an effervescence that gets its energy from a fatal-ist yet optimistic desire to foil fate. This marriage of hope and fear, of in-nocence and experience can best be understood as a deep response to long experience of high unemployment. Walter Hegarty expresses something of this in his first Derry novel, *The Price of Chips*. (From where we stand we can look directly across to the Waterside, and to the area where the story has its setting.) The opening paragraph (the book was published in 1973) hints at how the 'gale of the world', in the form of the troubles, was to impact upon the lives of the innocent and the unsuspecting: 'A gale struck the side of the house with the dull echoing thud of a giant carpet-beater and the urgent clamour of the rain at the window. Colm O'Kane left down the *Wizard*.'

And so, the age of innocence passes. The local takes on universal significance. Half a century earlier the novelist and poet Shane Leslie stood (in contradiction to his background) as a nationalist candidate in the 1910 Derry elections. He used this experience, in part, in his 1923 novel, *Doomsland* and also returned to it in his autobiography, *Long Shadows*, published in 1966. His description of the experience seems to me to catch the essential ambiguity of Irish affairs, as perceived by so many bemused observers. Firstly an acceptance of the nature of what is seen as essentially humorous, if lawless, but ultimately merely local, manners:

> Both sides voted the dead as well as the sick…an old man carried to the poll voted for me and died on the way back. I sent a wreath to his funeral…there was no trick, no fraud, no subtlety which either side would not play.

But quickly he comes to an awareness that this local skirmish is more – it is a scene from some universal battle. In Hegarty's terms a breeze, but a breeze deriving, indeed, from the great wind of the world:

> These were election times when invisible figures rise from the grave. If I was confronted by the thought that Patrick Sarsfield and Robert Emmet were on my side, I realised that behind each corner waited Oliver Cromwell and William of Orange. How could such mighty antagonists, descending like gods or Homer into battle, ever shake hands…

And round every corner in Derry the scene changes and with it the mood and tempo of life alters, and languages mirrors this kaleidoscope of light and life. Frances Molloy (whose sudden and tragic early death in 1991 robbed us of a unique voice) takes and uses language as a material to be juggled, whipped and spun into forms that unexpectedly leap off the page. In her hands, the written language is used in an attempt, as it were, to escape the mundane constraints of the formal sentence and as if in struggling aversion to the regularity of the daily grind. Set in a Derry factory (these distinctive buildings are all around, one stands not many yards from New Gate) the novel, despite its surface playfulness, is an unusually honest and essentially unromantic exploration of working-class experience, as seen through the eyes of a young woman. Where Hegarty's book reflects the overlapping reality of growing up within and between two religious communities, and of the creeping plague of sectarianism, Molloy takes on board another reality, this time the centrality of the shirt factory in Derry's financial and emotional economy, and the centrality of the role women have played as the main or only family breadwinner. This is a theme shouldered, with an unrepentant directness, on to the stage by Frank McGuinness in his early play, *The Factory Girls,* (set in the north west, it was first produced in Dublin in 1982). This is another work in which awareness of and felicity in working-class language forms a basic and constituent part.

A concern with language is often the initial motivating force with writers associated with Derry. Sometimes it takes a serious, distanced and cerebral form (yet rooted in a linguistic place and a community that is essentially working-class, as in the work of critic and poet Seamus Deane). Sometimes, although rising from a similar ground, it takes the form of poet Michael Foley's condensed and discontented humour. Sometimes it expresses the buried sombreness of Brian Friel who, in all of his work, but particularly so in the play *Translations,* exemplifies a long term, serious and sophisticated awareness of the nature and function of language, and of its relation to place and to time. In his work he repeatedly indicates a larger, but abstract, concern with the relationship between an organic culture and its political contexts – a concern made the more urgent given the 'gale of the world' that blows still across the hills. In this, both he and Hegarty are concerned with loss of innocence, and with the rigours imposed upon us as we grow to maturity in a harsh, adult world.

Just below us here, and clinging like ivy to the walled city, is a small estate of houses. The Fountain and its people have experienced many changes over the years. These have been recorded in a community book, *The Fountain,* written by the people of the area together with Leon McAuley. Published in 1993 by the Arts Council of Northern Ireland and the Verbal Arts Centre the book stands as a cogent and often moving piece of cultural history and as the expression and voice of an entire working-class community.

> And if you hadn't enough
> when you counted up
> you would say, 'Oh, God,
> I haven't much this week…'
> Then you'd have gone up
> and got more work
> and taken the tickets off
> and sewed them in.
> That was *dead horses.*
>
> That's what they called them,
> *dead horses,*
> because the work wasn't done
> to the next week.
> Then you went in on Monday morning
> and you had to kill yourself
> trying to get the *dead horses* done

before you started earning
for the Friday's wage.
It was just a vicious circle.
All the time you were working, trying too...'

'There were no times like them
all the same...'
'Not at all!'

We are still at New Gate, looking down over the rooftops of the Fountain and towards the bridge. This is as good a place as any to turn towards the inner walled city. Looking up London Street, we see on the right a fine building that now houses the Church of Ireland Diocesan Library and Offices. This ecclesiastical building (the library it houses is of some importance) stands on the site of an eighteenth century playhouse. Situated on the corner of Widow's Row (now London Street) and Artillery Lane (now Artillery Street), and known as 'The New Theatre', (it was Derry's second purpose-built theatre) it opened its doors during the autumn of 1789. However, the first production of which we have a record was *He Would be a Soldier* by Frederick Pilon, a Cork man. This took place on 5 January 1790 when the theatre hosted a gala evening, attended, splendid in their new uniforms, by the Derry Independent Volunteers.

On the opposite side of London Street the red brick Victorian Cathedral School building houses the Verbal Arts Centre, a cultural development project set up in 1992 to foster the local, regional and national heritage contained in the written and spoken verbal arts, and to encourage contemporary writing and storytelling. Behind that, standing in the Cathedral grounds, is a long, low building dedicated to the memory of the well known hymn writer Cecil Frances Alexander.

If one were to agree with D. H. Lawrence, when he insists in his essay *Hymns in a Man's Life*, on the enduring emotional and cultural importance of the hymns heard and sung in childhood, then Mrs Alexander is surely an important cultural figure. She was the author of a number of enduring and popular hymns, among which the best known are, 'There is a Green Hill Far Away' (it is highly likely that this is another reference to Derry's terrain), 'Once in Royal David's City' and 'All things Bright and Beautiful'. In the manner of her time, she was a very highly productive writer. While not primarily a poet, her extensive body of hymns and verse does contain pieces of merit. 'The Breastplate of St. Patrick', although owing much to an earlier Irish model, provides a good example of the simplicity and strength of diction of which she is capable, at her best. Her husband, William, also associated with St Columb's Cathedral, was born in Derry in 1824. He was to become Bishop of Derry, later Archbishop of Armagh and Primate of All Ireland, and was (almost) as equally a prolific creator of verse as his wife. His *Poems and Essays* was published in London in 1867.

Mrs Alexander is remembered in the cathedral by a stained glass window, and in the cathedral precincts by a plaque on the music-room wall. A fine portrait hangs in the Deanery on Bishop Street. Another and more entertaining testimony to her life and work is contained in her daughter, Eleanor Alexander's, account of her parents' lives. This is largely set in Derry, as are a number of Eleanor's novels, among them *Lady Anne's Walk* (1903), *The Rambling Rector* (1904) and *The Lady of the Well* (1906).

The gothic cathedral was built in 1628-33 by The Honourable The Irish Society. This is commemorated by an inscription cut in stone and set in the porch:

> If Stones could speake
> Then London's prayse
> Should sound who
> Built this church and
> Cittie from the grounde

Extensive improvements were carried out to the cathedral in 1887: the Right Rev. Dr. Alexander offered a prize of fifty pounds for the best ode written to commemorate the opening. The competition was won by J.T.C. Humphreys of Castlefin. His poem was published in pamphlet form in Dublin in 1887.

St Columb's Cathedral was distinguished, too, by an association with George Berkeley. Described as 'one of the intellectual pioneers of America', (he lived in Newport, Rhode Island for a number of years) Berkeley held the office of dean of the cathedral during the period 1724 to 1732. An important (and during his lifetime a sometimes controversial) philosopher and thinker, Berkeley's work continues to hold its place in the history of philosophical development. He was a friend of many of the leading literary figures of his generation, among them Steele, Addison, Pope and Swift. In 1725, he unexpectedly received half of the estate of Hester Van Homrigh, otherwise known as Swift's 'Vanessa'. Although Berkeley composed occasional verse, as a writer, he is most noted for the clarity and lucidity of his prose. His 'Dialogues between Hylas and Philonous', first published in 1713, may be regarded still as perhaps the finest example in English of the conduct of argument by dialogue.

The cathedral has played host to a number of powerful communicators; most notably, and at an earlier date than Berkeley, it provided a home to John Bramhall. Born in Yorkshire in 1594, Bramhall was nominated to the bishopric of Derry in 1634. He was later to become primate of the Irish Church and speaker of the Irish House of Lords. Bramhall was an energetic controversialist and a great polemic writer. He rebuked John Milton (to whom he referred, in the context of a discussion of writing skills, as a 'young novice halting') and carried out a heated debate with Hobbes on, among other things, the nature of freedom of will. His style has been described (and kindly so) as 'unusual'. A happily short but otherwise rather typically contorted line of his reads, 'You congregate heterogeneous matter and segregate that which is homogeneous'. His prose style apart, he is an important thinker and writer of his period, deeply conscious of and intellectually responsive to many matters that proved to be of continuing political and religious significance. Appropriately, the address at his burial was given by Jeremy Taylor, a man who, in sharp contrast, is noted for the simplicity of his writing style, and who in a final generous tribute said of Bramhall, 'He wrote many things fit to be read, and did very many things worthy to be written'.

In Palace Street, just off Bishop Street, is to be found the pretty church of St. Augustine's. John Samuel Bewley Monsell was curate here between 1836 and 1838. He was born in 1811 in the Waterside. His birthplace, St. Columb's, had been built by his seagoing grandfather. Today it houses a reconciliation centre and its grounds form a very attractive riverside municipal park that takes its name from the original house. Monsell, like Mrs Alexander, was a prolific maker of hymns and poems; his books, which ran to numerous editions, include, *Parish Musing* (7th Ed. 1863) and *The Passing Bell and other poems* (2nd Ed. 1869). William Makepeace Thackeray, who was born in the same year as Monsell, records in his *The Irish Sketch Book* (1843) the 'delightful hospitality' he received when he paid a visit to 'the pretty lodge of St Columb's' during his visit to Londonderry.

The Torrens family had links with that part of the city associated with the cathedral, and nearby streets. The family established itself in Ireland in 1690, after the battle of the Boyne; subsequently, various members held church livings. One was prebendary of Derry. Another was headmaster of Derry diocesan school. Robert Torrens was born in 1780; he was a political economist who developed theories that influenced the thinking of Peel. Torrens wrote two novels, *Celebia Choosing a Husband: a modern novel* (1809) and *The Victim of Intolerance, or the Hermit of Killarney: a catholic tale* (1814). Robert Torrens went to live in Australia; the river on which Adelaide is built is named after him.

This exploring and adventuring disposition is found in another writer who came from a similar culture. The poet, journalist and comic dramatist, Susanna Centlivre (Carroll) was born Susanna Freeman (in 1666 or 1667), of a plantation family that had lately come to Ireland, reputedly to escape political difficulties in England. It is likely that her father was involved in the business of one of the London companies. Her story, which is full of uncertainties, being given variously by different sources, is liberally imbued with the spirit of seventeenth century adventuring and romanticism. She ran away from home at the age of fifteen (one source has it that she was an orphan with both her parents dead, another that her father remarried after her mother's death and that she ran away to escape her stepmother's cruelty).

Somehow, she made her way from the north west of Ireland to Liverpool and from there to London. She obtained employment (picaresquely, dressed as a boy) and set off to Cambridge. Subsequently, she joined a company of strolling players, married, it is reputed, three times (it is claimed her first two husbands died as the result of fighting duels) and found time to write eighteen plays. *The Works of the Celebrated Mrs Centlivre* was published in three volumes in 1872. The actor David Garrick found one of his most popular roles in a Centlivre play. Her London home became a centre of literary social life. Despite her subsequent fame, at one period she found that she had to publish her work anonymously because of what she perceived to be 'a severe prejudice' against women writing for the theatre.

The dramatist George Farquhar (whose family home was to the west of the city, in County Donegal) went to school near the walls here (in Society Street, just opposite what is now the Apprentice Boys' Hall) when he was a boarder at the Free School.

Now on Bishop Street, if we walk towards the Diamond we pass premises associated with the Coyle family. Kathleen Coyle, whose family had connections with Glendermott in the Waterside, was an author whose work achieved great popularity in England and America during the 1940s. She published thirteen novels. One, *A Flock of Birds,* came second to E. M. Forster's *A Passage to India* in a 1930 literary competition. Among her best books is her autobiographical account of a Derry childhood, *The Magical Realm* (1943). This deals with growing up in a large middle-class Derry family at the end of the nineteenth century and is particularly good at presenting the experiences and daily lives of women in that society. She has an eye for detail and an instinctive recourse to vivid imagery, as in this account of the annual burning of Lundy's effigy (an event that still takes place each year in Bishop Street):

> When it was almost dark enough for the moon to come out…high up in a place where the poor stuffed man swung on his gibbet, a star appeared. It stayed poised, waiting for the wind to swing Lundy towards it. As soon as his feet touched it it went off like a meteor and the blaze began. The traitor hung in the heavens like a lantern. He burned with his feet upwards. All his joints went off with cracks and explosions; and rags and tatters fell down in awful, ghostly wisps upon our faces. The more he burned the more he exploded.

Although her domestic circumstances were anything but serene, Coyle enjoyed an extremely rich, varied and eventful career. After leaving Derry she lived in other parts of Ireland as well as in England, Europe and America and was associated with the Suffragette and Labour movements. Today, Coyle's books are out of print and her work is hardly remembered. This is the fate of the work of two other women writers who have associations with Derry. The first was Mary Balfour, thought to have been born in January 1775. She was the daughter of a clergyman who was a close friend of the famous Earl Bishop Hervey of Derry. Mary published two books: the first in 1910, *Hope : a Poetical Essay with Various Other Poems* (which has a poem dedicated to the 'Earl of Bristol, Late Bishop of Derry'). This volume also contained *Kathleen O'Neill; a Poem* . The poem takes as its theme the tradition that one of the ladies of the O'Neill family had been carried away by the *Bean-Sigh* or *Banshee*. Later she produced a verse drama (described in its publicity material, somewhat ominously, as a 'grand national melodrama'). Confusingly this takes the name *Kathleen O'Neill*; one of the central characters is Phelim O'Neill, Prince of Ulster. The play was first produced in the Belfast Theatre in 1814 and was published in the same year. Mary Balfour's literary interests were wide and she set words to old Irish airs. Some of these were later used by Bunting. Together with her friend Mary Ann McCracken, she was one of the 191 original members of the Belfast Harp Society. Mary Balfour was part of that seeking and questioning generation that helped to awaken and educate the cultural perceptions of, among others, the poet Samuel Ferguson. At a later date Honoria Galwey – born in the Waterside in 1830 – was actively involved in collecting and recording traditional song and music, particularly in Derry and Donegal. She published *Old Irish Croonauns and other Tunes* in 1910. Her work influenced the Glens of Antrim poet Moira O'Neill.

The second writer, Anna McClure Warnock, was educated in the city and later at Girton College, Oxford. She wrote short stories and equally short plays; the latter were collected and published as the (undated), *Ulster Playlets* and *More Ulster Playlets (Ulsterettes)* and became extremely popular with London audiences, being regularly performed there by the Irish Literary Society. During the 1940s she wrote a great number of one act plays specially for amateur dramatic groups. Among her Belfast publications of this period are, *The Way of a Woman and other Ulster Sketches*, *The Wee Stones* and *New Ulster Playlets*.

We have seen the location of Derry's second theatre and, later in our journey, when we reach the quay side, we shall come upon the site of Derry's first theatre. Apart from those events which took place in purpose-built theatres, the city experienced considerable theatrical activity during the eighteenth century. The first recorded visit by a professional company of actors – the Smock Alley troupe from Dublin – took place in 1741. They may well have performed in the Town House or Exchange, a building situated in the Diamond (the market place), and which had been presented to the city by King William III. Being centrally situated the town house served a number of purposes, among them the provision of entertainment. Well before that date we have evidence of 'street theatre' in the city: William Edmundson, a Quaker preacher who visited Londonderry in the mid 1650s, records in his *Journal* (1715) how, when he came across a crowd of people watching 'actors and rope dancers', he seized the opportunity to take advantage of what, for him, was a ready-made congregation:

> I stood still and declared truth to them, directing them to the light of Christ in their own hearts, and they were very sober and attentive, but the stage players [and rope dancers] were sore vexed that the people left them, and followed me: whereupon they got the mayor to send two officers to take me to prison.

And to prison he went. Someone who would have known this area of the city was John Wilson, Recorder of Londonderry He was born in England (his place of birth is sometimes given as Yorkshire, sometimes as London). On coming to Ireland he was admitted to the Inner Temple in 1646 and called to the Bar in 1654. Wilson was appointed Recorder of Londonderry in 1666, a position he held until his resignation in 1680. It is probable that it was during his time in Derry that he wrote the tragicomedy, *Belphegor* (?1677). The play is based on Machiavelli's story of how Satan took the form of a married man to test the nature (or ill-nature) of wives.

John Wilson wrote five plays and one long poem (the latter was published in Dublin in 1682). His most popular work was *The Cheats* (1671); this received numerous performances and ran to many editions. Wilson's experience in Derry was enriched by various disputes with the local 'Puritans'. He is believed to have died in England in 1695 or 1696.

A short walk from the Diamond, turning left along Butcher Street and through Butcher Gate, and we find ourselves looking out over the Bogside. Holding the flat ground between the walled city and Creggan hill this area has associations with at least two writers. These are the journalist Eamonn McCann, whose book *War in an Irish Town* (1974) provides an account of the Bogside and Derry during the early seventies, and Nell McCafferty who was born into the immediately postwar Bogside with its interrelated network of little streets. Journalist, columnist and author Nell McCafferty, has published five books, including the novel, *Peggy Deery* (1988). Set in the Creggan, and subtitled 'A Family at War', this is another instructive account of a working-class Derry woman's life, and of the community and social context in which she finds herself.

At this point, Free Derry Corner is below us and immediately to our left. The gable end of a building, now having the status of a community icon, it stands securely beside a range of varied new buildings, mostly fine town houses that shelter the rising generations. This complicated interconnectedness of historical fact, of physical and cultural significance and of family and community relationships, sets the place shivering in response to even the slightest touch of the exploring imagination. It is this combination of emotion and rational consciousness that acts as a form of powerhouse for the creative imagination and that provides the energy for a work such as *Peggy Deery* or, indeed, for the energetic language of the community book *The Fountain,* previously mentioned.

As we retrace our steps back into the historic city centre it is intriguing to remember that, two centuries before Kathleen Coyle was born, one George Douglas, printer and bookseller, had premises here in the Diamond. Douglas was an industrious man who, as printer, publisher and later editor, holds a still largely unacknowledged place in the history of provincial printing and newspaper history.

Continuing down Shipquay Street we pass on our right the bank building on the first floor of which the fine novelist Joyce Cary was born on 7 December, 1888. Going through the gates, immediately on our left we can see the Guildhall. This occupies, almost exactly, the site of Derry's first purpose-built theatre. Erected in 1774, the Ship Quay Theatre opened on the 8th August with the double bill of *The Constant Couple*, a comedy by George Farquhar, and *The Deuce Is in Him,* a farce by George Coleman. Never intended as a permanent fixture the building became dangerous (structurally damaged one evening, it is said, as a result of shaking caused by the excessive laughter of a much-moved audience). Following on from some eighteenth century local arts politics Ship Quay Theatre was replaced by The New Theatre, already referred to, and built near New Gate. No physical trace of the old theatre remains but, by one of those quirks of history for which Ireland is famous, it was on this same piece of ground that, two hundred years later, Brian Friel chose to set his 1973 play, *The Freedom of the City.*

Derry has the immense good fortune to lie among hills and between two great waterways, the Foyle and the Swilly. The Swilly has inspired creative activity. Known, and appropriately so, lying as it does in the lea of blue and brown mountains, and under the ever-changing clouds of the western skies, as the 'Lake of Shadows', it has drawn poetry from people such as Percy French and Mrs Alexander. Both waterways have played their part in the political and social history of Derry and the north west. The Swilly provided the pathway for the Flight of the Earls. The event inspired Alfred Perceval Graves to write a poem of leave taking:

> To other shores across the sea
> We speed with swelling sails.

Much later, it was on Swilly's waters that Wolfe Tone was captured. Not to be outdone in historical reference, the Foyle can claim the breaking of the boom in 1689 (a turning point in the siege of Derry). This event, together with the Foyle's importance to the city, inspired another piece of verse. This time from Charlotte E. Tonna, and to the air of 'Cailín Donn'.

> Where Foyle his swelling waters,
> Rolls northwards to the main
> Here, Queen of Erin's daughters
> Fair Derry fixed her reign
> A rampart wall around her,
> The river at her feet.

And equally importantly, for centuries the Foyle was a place of emigration and immigration, of many waves of leavings and returnings. The two waterways have been important, both as channels of communication and as barriers to inter-group commerce. For centuries, they have held significance as tribal borders. And, from humble beginnings that broaden out into wide sea loughs, both waterways display great, though very different, forms of beauty. In a poem attributed to St Columba he describes the arousal of his feelings on entering the Foyle on a return trip to Derry.

> We are rounding Moy-n-Olung, we sweep by its head, and
> We plunge through Lough Foyle
> Whose swans would enchant with their music the dead, and
> Make pleasure of toil.

On a different theme, this time very much in the mode of realism, for he himself had undertaken the journeys he describes, the west Donegal novelist Patrick MacGill viewed the quay side where we now find ourselves as a solemn place – a spot associated in folk memory with rites of passage, largely of enduring departure, though sometimes of return. But, and this is where the Foyle stands in contradistinction to the rural Swilly, he depicts it as a place of great social vitality also, with the outgoing emigrants crowding into the popular and noisy eating place, the 'Donegal House' or 'shaking their feet' as they dance away their waiting time in the quayside pub. The bustle of human commerce always grabs his attention and in his 1915 novel, *The Rat Pit,* he describes the scene on a boat carrying men and women going off to seek work in Scotland.

> The boat was crowded with harvestmen from Frosses,
> potato-diggers from Glenmornan and Gweedore, cattle drov-
> ers from Coleraine and Londonderry, second-hand clothes
> dealers, bricklayers, labourers, farm hands, young men and
> old, women and children; all sorts and conditions of people.

Another novelist, William Makepeace Thackeray, on a visit to the city in the middle of the previous century, also found the streets near the Foyle full of vigour and life. In his account of his experience he presents a scene distinguished by noise, movement and industry. Thackeray praised the city, finding that, 'The public buildings of Derry are, I think, among the best I have seen in Ireland; and the lunatic Asylum, especially, is to be pointed out as a model of neatness and comfort'. Asylum Road, which we now approach, runs off at right angles from the river, and is part of a little complex of streets that includes Lawrence Hill and Great James Street. Lawrence Hill was where Norah McGuinness, the accomplished and progressive landscape painter and book illustrator, was born in 1903. McGuinness studied in Dublin, London and Paris. She worked in New York and in London (during this time, mostly engaged on book illustration) before returning to Dublin. She provided illustrations for *The Dublin Magazine,* the most important literary magazine of the period. She also did work for W.B. Yeats. Among other exhibitions, her work was shown in Derry's Brooke Park Gallery in 1969 and again at the city's Keys Gallery in 1976. Norah McGuinness was deeply involved in the Irish Exhibition of Living Art and was an honorary member of the Royal Hibernian Academy.

Great James Street was the birthplace of the literary critic D. E. S. Maxwell. He was educated at Foyle College. Maxwell has published studies of Eliot, Yeats and of American fiction, including the first major assessment of the work of the novelist James Gould Cozzens (1903-78). His *Poets of the Thirties* (1969) has become an essential text for serious students of twentieth century literature in English. He has also written a book on Irish drama; his *Brian Friel* (1973) was the first full length study to be devoted to the writer and his work.

If, before leaving the quayside area, we turn and look directly across the river we can see Ebrington Barracks where the poet Francis Ledwidge was stationed for a period of time during the First World War. An Irish nationalist by sympathy, and tending towards the left by conviction (he had been involved in initiating the labour movement in County Meath), Ledwidge joined the British Army (partly, it appears, as a way of getting over a broken love affair) and served with the Royal Inniskilling Fusiliers at Gallipoli and then on the Western Front. A romantic by instinct, and although not a 'political' writer, Ledwidge was a self-educated man whose power as a poet grew as he moved away from pastoral imagery and towards a rather more rigorous response to social experience. Yet, in one of his most moving poems, 'Lament for the Poets: 1916', he turns naturally and with great effect to the topography of Derry:

> I heard a Poor Old Woman say:
> 'At break of day the fowler came,
> And took my blackbirds from their songs
> Who loved me well thro' shame and blame.
>
> But in the lonely hush of eve
> Weeping I grieve the silent bills.'
> I heard the Poor Old Woman say
> In Derry of the little hills.

When, while on foreign soil, the soldier and poet Siegfried Sassoon's thoughts turned to the essence of England (the images and sounds of cricket) the poet and soldier Ledwidge turned his thoughts to the essence of Ireland, and to the rural landscape around Derry. 'By Faughan' (written during or just after a period in hospital in Egypt in 1916, and 'for hills and woods and streams unsung') is a poem that celebrates the inspiration found in memory and place, the 'trysting place of beauty and beauty':

> Twixt wind and silence Faughan flows,
> In music broken over rocks,
> Like mingled bells the poet knows
> Ring in the fields of Eastern flocks.
> And here the song for you I find
> Between the silence and the wind.

Ebrington Barracks has another literary connection. It was from here that Charles John McGuinness escaped custody (and later departed the city dressed as a priest). McGuinness was born in Lower Road, off William Street, in 1893, although much of his childhood was spent at 19 Meadowbank Avenue. An amazingly colourful character who lead an equally amazing, varied and colourful life, McGuinness sums up the exotic peaks of his own experience in the subtitle to his book, *Nomad: Memoirs of an Irish sailor, soldier, pearl-fisher, pirate, gunrunner, rebel and Antarctic explorer* (1934). McGuinness was awarded the Congressional Gold Medal for his part in the Byrd expedition to the Antarctic; he was involved in gunrunning from Germany to Ireland during the War of Independence; he brought an Indian princess home to meet his family; and so on. Stories abound about the captain. Charles John McGuinness died at sea during the winter of 1947.

Turning from the River Faughan to the Foyle, if we were to follow the river's course we would quickly gain an impression of having left the city, for here one is never far from the country. Numerous little roads lead out from the urban density and up into the hills, where they network into tangled webs, often to be unexpectedly and rudely dissected by the meandering border. We have noted how Sean O'Faolain linked writer to landscape; in an intimate relationship between Irish writer and place the very earth becomes a cultural seismograph, recording both the positive and the negative tremors caused by human action. Looking eastwards across this border, responding to such a pastoral landscape, the Donegal poet Francis Harvey has written:

> Beside this Ulster road flanked
> with grass banks and summer flowers
> the print of last night's lovers
> brings the soldiers running running.

This to me is one of the most understated and delicately balanced expressions of how violence cankers innocence and perverts our very perceptions.

But we must now turn aside from the river and move uphill towards Northland Road.

Just off Northland Road, which runs parallel to the Strand Road, lies Crawford Square, an oasis of trees set around a formally hedged lawn. This was the site of the Victoria High School for Girls (it was later to become Londonderry High School for Girls, and later still to form part of Foyle and Londonderry College). Norah McGuinness was educated here, as was Ellie Stewart (who published one volume of poetry, *From a Ballycastle Garden* (1944). Stewart is remembered for her activities as a suffragist. This was a passion she shared with Kathleen Coyle. Margaret Gillespie (Cousins) is another Victoria High School girl who was involved in radical politics. She organised Sylvia Pankhurst's visit to Derry in 1910. Her autobiography, *We Two Together*, was published in 1950. When one considers these women, together with others mentioned here, one sees an emerging pattern. It is of independently minded women, interested in giving individual voice to their experiences. But, more than that, they share a desire to challenge and to bring about social and political improvements.

Northland Road is home too to Magee College, itself home, if fitfully, to both creative and critical bursts of activity of a literary kind. From here was published *Acorn*, a journal published by the English Department. In its seventeen issues, produced between 1961 and 1972, it provided a platform for a wide variety of writers. These ranged from Walter Allen to Francis Stuart, from Brendan Kennelly to W. R. Rodgers and from Seamus Heaney to George MacBeth. *Acorn* was edited by Professor Alan Warner, a specialist in Anglo-Irish writing and one of the few who attended early to, and wrote with innovative sympathy about, the work of John Hewitt and Patrick Kavanagh. The college had close associations with Barbara Hunter (Edwards). She published, *Who'll Carry the Bag:* a comedy after the *Kremer Korb* of Hans Sachs in 1950. As well as having an interest in drama, Barbara Hunter acted as coeditor of the Ulster literary quarterly, *Rann* (1948-1953), an interesting and important publication that shared in the strong regional explorations that many progressive thinkers, and in particular, writers, were then engaging in, in Ireland, Scotland, Wales and parts of England. Among many others, *Rann* published the work of Robert Greacen, the Derry-born poet and editor. His books include the (1944) *Northern Harvest*, one of the first collections devoted to Ulster writing. Greacen, who was born at 57 Bennett Street left Derry in 1925. He returned nearly seventy years later:

> A stranger among strangers
> I look for my house of birth.
> *Pulled down years ago.*
> I show the paper: 'I certify...'

Ich bin ein Derryman
A stranger grips my hand.

I moon at the Guildhall
Buy postcards, a newspaper,
Watch armoured cars
Patrolling history.

This poem of 'homecoming' was first published in *Poetry Ireland Review*, No 34. Though primarily a poet (he has published some five volumes of verse) Greacen was also involved in editing two influential anthologies in the 1940s – *Lyra: A Book of New Lyrics*, coedited with Alex Comfort, and the *Faber Contemporary Irish Verse*, coedited with Valentin Iremonger. *Even Without Irene* (1969) is an autobiographical account of his early life. His collected poems are due to be published during 1994.

The important Ulster dialect poet W.F. Marshall had personal and family connections with the college. At a later date Magee was home for a period of time to the Welsh novelist, Mary Jones, to poet Hugh Maxton (better known, perhaps, as the literary critic W.J. McCormack), to poet Andrew Waterman and before that to the critic and teacher Terence Brown, who studied there. He was a contemporary of the poet and broadcaster Rory Brennan who was for a period secretary of the national poetry organisation, *Poetry Ireland*. Brennan published two collections, *The Sea on Fire* (1979), for which he received the Patrick Kavanagh Award and *The Walking Wounded* (1985). Magee College also has a connection with the writer Nik Cohn. Now living and working in America, he is the author of a substantial history of popular music and the winner of the 1993 Thomas Cook Travel Award. Cohn spent his childhood in Derry, where his father taught at the college.

Norman Cohn was Professor of French at Magee between 1951 and 1960. In 1957 he published his influential book on cultural and sociological history, *The Pursuit of the Millennium: revolutionary Millenarians and Mystical Anarchists of the Middle Ages*. This book went through various editions in English, and has been translated in French, German, Japanese, Spanish and Italian. Cohn left Magee in 1960 to take up the post of Director of the Columbus Centre at Sussex University; he was General Editor of the Centre's *Studies in Persecution and Extermination* during the period 1966 to 1988. In 1967 he received the Anisfield-Wolf Award in Race Relations.

A graduate of Magee who later published a novel about student life in Ulster during the late 1960s is Elizabeth Gibson. *The Water is Wide* (1984) is recognisably set in the college; within the framework of the wider social and political context of the late sixties it examines student life from a Christian perspective. Greta Mulrooney, another graduate of Magee, had her first novel short-listed for the East Midlands Arts Heinemann Award and has published a children's book, *A Can of Worms* (1993). Sean McMahon, who studied at the college, has a number of children's books to his credit. We can note here two other Derry writers who have published children's fiction. Maeve Friel, originally from the Waterside but now living in England, has two novels to her credit and at the time of writing has a third at an advanced stage. Friel has been the recipient of a Hennessy award for prose. Kathy Campbell, originally from Pennyburn and now living in New York, has published children's prose. Her book, *Demons of the Woods* (1993) received a literary award in America. I have discussed how a natural love of language is reflected in a significant proportion of writing from the city. This manifests itself at an early age, and two collections of children's street rhymes have been made and published – *Slide Down my Rainbow* by Sheila Quigley (1993) and *1, 2, 3, O'Leary* by Jim Craig (1994).

To return to Magee: the college has proved to be a cultural magnet, drawing many writers into Derry. This was so in the days of *Acorn*, but was particularly so during that period in the 1970s when R. D. Smith, Professor of Liberal Studies, sometime (award-winning) drama producer with the BBC and husband of the novelist Olivia Manning, attracted a vital and colourful caravan of famous contributors to an extensive programme of literary readings and lectures. In this he was actively supported by F.J. D'Arcy who, before taking up a career in adult education, did work for Radio Telefís Éireann, was editor of the Dublin journal *Hibernia* and literary editor of the *Irish Independent*.

At a different level of intensity, Magee College, through a joint WEA and university extra mural studies programme, played host for many years to the very active Writers' Workshop. One of the first such ventures in supporting community writing in Northern Ireland (the first workshop was offered jointly by R. D. Smith and Sam Burnside in 1974) it provided an important form of innovative encouragement for new creative and imaginative writing during the seventies and eighties and gave many local and aspiring writers their first public platform. Among those involved were two local writers who have gone on to publish books for children, Jack Scoltock and Mary Regan. Among others who have had their imaginative work broadcast, published or performed are Myra Dryden, Frank Galligan, Danny Gorman, Eddie Kerr, Tessa Johnston, Cahir O'Doherty, Dave Duggan and Jack Houlahan. Houlahan's Radio Four play, *Maiden City Magic,* was selected as the BBC's entry for the 1993 *Prix Italia* radio drama award. *Borderlines* (1988), edited by Sam Burnside and with an introduction by Frank McGuinness, contained representative samples of contemporary work by north west writers.

As well as nurturing local talent the Writers' Workshop, and its offshoot the *Writer to Writer* scheme, acted as a magnet, attracting visiting speakers of the stature of the poet Michael Longley and the novelist, poet, critic and Professor of Creative Writing at Lancaster University, David Craig. In promoting a continuing dialogue between the local community and writers of note, the impressive list of visitors grew to include novelists, poets and playwrights such as Jennifer Johnston, Medbh McGuckian and Christina Reid and William Trevor, literary editors such as David Marcus and columnists like the *Observer's* Sue Arnold.

Still on the Northland Road, by proceeding a little further we come to Foyle and Londonderry College. The college is descended from the school attended by Farquhar during the siege. (William) Percy French, the writer whose lyrics (among these is 'The Mountains of Mourne') are known worldwide was educated here. R. W. K. Edwards, who taught at the school in the 1880s, wrote a novel that adopts the siege of Derry as its background. J.B. Bury the distinguished classical scholar and historian was educated at Foyle College. Initially drawn to poetry (he had a great appetite for reading and an equally great facility for memorising verse) his career led him first to the study of classical philology, then philosophy and finally history. The published bibliography of his writings contains three hundred and sixty nine entries. Among these is *The Life of St Patrick and his place in history* (1905), an edition of Gibbon's *Decline and Fall*, complete with notes and appendices (the first volume was published in 1896, the seventh and last in 1900) and *A History of Freedom of Thought* (1914). R.I. Best is another Foyle pupil who went on to achieve remarkable success. He was assistant director and later director of the National Library of Ireland, chairman of the Irish Manuscripts Commission and an honorary fellow of the Bibliographical Society of Ireland. Among his publications are *The Irish Mythological Cycle and Celtic Mythology* (1903) and the *Bibliography of Irish Philology and Manuscripts Literature Publications* (1942). Best was awarded the Leibniz Medal of the Royal Prussian Academy, one of the highest distinctions in international scholarship.

We are never far from history in Londonderry and the place has produced at least one historian of exceptional merit. F. S. L. Lyons was born in the city on the 11 November 1923. The eldest son of a bank manager, Stewart Lyons, he was educated first in England and later in Dublin. Lyons contributed greatly to intellectual life in Ireland: he was an outstanding historian, biographer and teacher, as well as being a pioneering cultural critic. He was one of the first to take as his critical text the importance of our recognising the political need to deal with the challenges inherent in cross-community coexistence. He articulated his thesis in terms of cultural diversity and cultural unity. He was troubled by, as he put it, 'the disconnections in our history between politics and culture'. Lamenting the lack of detailed attention given to an understanding of literature's revealing potential, he went on to quote Estyn Evans: 'I believe that the personality of society is a powerful motive force and that it finds expression in the cultural landscape' (in the 1978 W.B. Rankin memorial lecture, 'The Burden of Our

History' given at Queens University). This is of particular interest when taken in conjunction with O'Faolain's remarks about Derry. It underpins Lyons's growing concern (evident, for example, in his book, *Culture and Anarchy in Ireland 1890-1939*) that we in Ireland should assume more comfortably the weight of our history by achieving a better understanding of the complexity of our many-stranded culture and by striving for greater knowledge of our imaginative and written heritages.

We now come to the place James Simmons was born: one mile north of the city at the junction of a side road that leads to Fahan, (itself a place of poets). He lived here in a house known as 'Greengables' before his family moved closer to the city (to 82 Northland Road). Simmons has played an important part in the literary life of Northern Ireland and is a central figure, though never quite of the 'establishment' (literary or otherwise). He has written much, taught in secondary and higher education and has engaged in innovative publishing activities. In the late sixties he started the seminal periodical, the *Honest Ulsterman*, described in its early years as a *monthly handbook for a revolution*, an indication of Simmons's ever-present desire to test the given, whether it be emotional or rational, private or public.

If we continue on along the Northland Road, passing 'Greengables', and turning right on to the Buncrana Road we come to St Columb's College, now removed, in part, from its old site on Bishop Street (without the walls), to a modern redbrick building. So far as literature is concerned, St Columb's is associated famously with the names of Seamus Heaney, Seamus Deane and Brian Friel. Each has been professionally concerned with language, imagination and society. Individually, each of these men has played a highly significant role in the imaginative and creative life of the island. Collectively, most notably through their part in the founding of Field Day, they have sought to influence both serious and popular cultural thinking about the political dynamics of the literary imagination.

The college has associations with other writers. Teacher, Paul Wilkins has published one volume of poetry *Pasts* (1979) while former pupil Michael Foley has published a number of volumes of poetry, including *Heil Hitler* (1969), *The Acne and the Ecstasy* (1971), *True Life Love Stories* (1976), *The Go Situation* (1982) and *Insomnia in the Afternoon* (1994). In this his customary humour is poised against what is at times an almost barbarous truth-telling, both about self and others. Foley has written one volume of prose fiction, *The Passion of Jamesie Coyle* (1978). Sean McMahon taught at the St Columb's for many years. He has done much to stimulate popular interest in Irish literary and historical matters, not least by producing a number of books designed to make these areas accessible to a wider audience. He has also written two books for children, *The Light on Illancrone* (1990) and *The Three Seals* (1991). Together with Art Ó Broin (long resident in Derry) and Brian Walker he compiled and edited *The Faces of Ireland* (1980). He also edited *The Best of the Bell* (1978). The college has associations with Phil Coulter who, although primarily a creator and maker of music, has written song lyrics. Most notably, given the writer's connection with Derry, the well-known, 'The Town I Love So Well'.

A little further along this road and we come to the offices of the *Derry Journal*. The very first issue of what was then called the *Derry Journal and General Advertiser* was produced by G. Douglas at his premises in the Diamond on Wednesday 3 June 1772, making it one of the longest established newspapers in Ireland. The paper has an honourable history of support for creative writing. Late in 1788 Douglas conceived the idea of establishing a poetry competition to commemorate the centenary of the siege. He published the winning piece in December of the same year, and in 1781 reproduced it together with a selection of other entries in the oddly-titled volume, *The Poliorciad*. Almost two hundred years later *The Derry Journal* published Patrick MacGill's early work.

Coming to the junction of the Buncrana and Muff roads a left turn would take us to Thornhill College. It was here that Kathleen Ferguson was educated. Her novel *The Maid's Tale* (1994) is set in Derry during the period 1957 to the early 1990s. In it she deals with themes of expression, identity and power. A central concern in the novel is an exploration of how language is intimately related to these things. *The Maid's Tale* displays the same awareness of and attention to the significance of language that we have noted in the work of other Derry writers. And, in important ways, Ferguson has used her perception of language to extend their concerns: viewing it in both its function as metaphor and as literal vehicle, in this novel she begins to examine how the cultural imperialism of language can be subverted in a creative and positive way, and in a manner that underpins the vitality and richness of the vernacular.

The novelist Jennifer Johnston lives not far from here, slightly to the north and close to 'the new bridge over the Foyle that sings perpetually', (as Michael Foley has it in his poem 'Talking to God on the new bridge over the Foyle'). She lives just off the Culmore Road at a place where the spreading city meets the country; her home is a house set in the formality of mature park-lands and riverside gardens. The river flows to the front of the house; here the ships passed within hailing distance three hundred years ago on their way to break the siege of Derry. Behind her house, middle-class Derry spreads out in ever-extending new housing estates (here you see signposts leading to Drummond Park and Griffith Park, so named in honour of the men who led the great Ordnance Survey). It seems appropriate that Jennifer Johnston should live and work in such a location, cocooned quietly behind a bounding stone wall. (Many of the distinctive stone walls to be found in Ireland were built in the nineteenth century as part of extensive famine relief schemes: others were constructed to mark the boundaries of large estates laid out during and after the plantations of Ireland. Some, at least, of the walls here may predate the famine by at least a century.) Jennifer

Johnston is imaginatively productive in the context of such historical, social, cultural and architectural diversity. Since 1972 she has been producing novels that deal with the consequences of diversity – and the changes that that implies, including the impact of difference on mono-cultures – whether this be through the medium of age, class or culture. And she had done so in language that has been honed against a model of classical economy. Her work stands comfortably beside that of the best discussed elsewhere in this book. Her husband, David Gilliland, combines a love of travel with the art of the photographer. His photographs have had public showings in two exhibitions mounted by the Gordon Galleries.

We now return to the city, along the Strand Road. As its name implies this road runs parallel to the river. On the corner of Strand Road and Lawrence Hill stands the North West Institute of Further and Higher Education, formerly known as the Technical College. Angela Doherty (née Tuckett) was a student here; before that she had been a pupil at Long Tower Primary School. She has written under three names: Doherty, O'Neill and Petron. As Angela Doherty she published *Constant Friends* in 1993. A modern historical novel it is set mainly in Derry and Donegal during the period 1958 till 1969. As Angela Petron she has published a series of popular light suspense novels. These usually have well-researched foreign backgrounds. Finally, as Angela O'Neill she has written *Flames on the Hill* (1993), a heavily researched historical novel that takes as its source nineteenth century evictions in Donegal.

Increasingly now, we have intermittent views of the rising city walls. No visitor to Derry, much less any of its residents, can ignore its magnificent stone walls with their four main gates and their heavy, flanking bastions. For the Protestant community in particular the walls continue to provide a strong cultural and emotional link to the past.

We enter the city by Shipquay Gate. Just on the wall here is a tablet erected to the memory of the breaking of the boom on the Foyle. This was a significant event in the siege, a crucial point at which the besieged were relieved by supply ships. The *Mountjoy*, captained by Michael Browning, crashed through the boom, or barrier, erected across the river. Captain Browning, a local man, died in the incident.

The siege of Derry, taken as both historical event and as cultural symbol, has stimulated a potentially significant if now largely overlooked body of writing of an imaginative kind. More celebratory than critical, more descriptive than analytical, its importance lies in two things. Firstly, it is useful for the ways in which it throws complementary light on the various better known factual historical records. These include a number of contemporaneous and documentary accounts, some of which take diary form. Secondly, this singular body of work is of great interest for the ways in which those who turned their hands to poetry, drama and the novel, allow us to see and examine the temper of the Protestant mind. This aspect of these imaginative creations demonstrates the universal, and in some important ways the radical, nature of the protesting concerns, shifting their drama out of the purely local and placing it on a world stage.

Of this body of work, two pieces are of particular interest. Aickin's long poem *Londerias: or a narrative of the Siege of Londonderry in verse* was published in Dublin in 1699. Little is known of Aickin – he may have been a doctor present at the siege – but his poem chronicles in detail the actions and the actors in the drama. Colonel John Mitchelburne was governor of Derry for a period of time during the siege. Despite its ultimately successful outcome, he himself did not gain from the event. His family was decimated and he incurred substantial personal debts. Unable to pay these, he returned to London where he was thrown into the Fleet prison where he wrote a play. *Ireland Preserved, or the Siege of Derry* (1705) was written, partly at least, in an attempt to explain and support his own position and claim to recompense, partly, perhaps, to earn some money. (It has been suggested that he was helped in his writing by George Farquhar, but this is not proven.) The play became extremely popular in Ireland, and was repeatedly reprinted in provincial towns. It enjoyed frequent performance in unlikely places, including rural barns and sheds. Carleton, in his account of his early life, mentions having seen it performed in a barn in the Clogher valley.

The siege and the relief of Derry have provided the subject matter and inspiration for at least twelve novels, five plays and well over forty poems. The plays were in the main contemporaneous, appearing just after the event, while the novels, apart from two published early in the twentieth century, are of the nineteenth century. The poetry spans a period of three hundred years. This is a significant body of imaginative work, having an identity arising out of one of the seminal and by now securely established symbolic events in Ireland's history. It has provided strongly bonded emotional and mental associations that have entered into and coloured language at a popular level of usage. Connotations of the term 'siege' (both as a physical and as a psychological manifestation) and of the nature of defence, are frequently used. Highly charged definitions of the terms of 'friend' and 'foe' appear in this literature. An understanding of the importance of this grows when it is translated in political contexts into the tribal 'us' and 'them'. These issues together with powerful associations relating to group solidarity and individual freedom of belief, conscience, thought and action, imbue much of this body of work, making it a useful mirror to some of the cultural convictions held today. (A discussion of the significance of this material, together with an extensive bibliography, can be found in, Sam Burnside, 'No temporising with the foe; literary materials relating to the Siege of Derry', *The Linenhall Review*, Vol. 5, No. 3, Autumn 1988, pp 4–9.)

In its various aspects the 'Siege and Relief', while overtly 'belonging' to the Protestant community, provides a series of metaphors that have proved to be persistent and useful for both traditions, and for those in Derry and those further afield. Thomas Carnduff, the Belfast shipyard labourer who wrote on working-class issues and themes, presents the Protestant perception of the symbol neatly here, with its implicit faith in reliance on self and a concurrent suspicion of external authority:

> 'Boys,' cried Irwin, 'if Antrim's men enter that gate, Derry is doomed. There are none in authority in this city who have the courage to stand forth and defend the place. Are we to stand by without striking a blow for the protection of our homes, and to see the liberties we now possess taken from us? I for one' – and he drew his sword as he spoke – 'will willingly die in defence of my people and my faith.'
> 'And I – and I – and I,' came voice after voice, till the thirteen stood ranked together.
> 'Then close the gates and man the walls', shouted Alex Irwin.

It is of some interest that the imaginative material arising out of the siege is not better known though, in literary terms it, must be admitted, much of it is of its time and without any outstanding aesthetic or wholly literary merit. Nevertheless, as one potentially accessible and valuable expression of a dynamic and richly complex culture it deserves rather more serious exploration than it has attracted to date.

Colonel George Philips, who had been governor of Derry in King Charles II's time, was invited to take on once again the responsibility during the reign of James II. He resigned after a short period of time to be replaced by the ill-fated Lundy (Lundy's name in Ireland has entered into popular language usage and is still synonymous with treachery). Our interest in him lies with his son, William Philips who was the author of a number of plays. One of these was produced at Dublin's Smock Alley theatre in 1699 or 1700. It was published by John Brocas in School House Lane in 1700 under the title *St Stephen's Green: or, The Generous Lovers.* Although the piece is no more than typical of its time (it is a Restoration 'manners' play) it is distinguished in one important respect: it is the earliest example of a play by an Irish writer that depicts local people on the stage. That this was a conscious decision on Philips' part, arising out of a pride in what he accepted as his Irish heritage, is indicated in his dedication.

Our journey has now brought us back to the city walls with their many and various associations. Behind these stone ramparts John Mitchel, author of *Jail Journal,* spent a year when he worked in the city as a clerk. Mitchel was admired by Edward Walsh, author of the haunting, 'The Dawning of the Day'. This is one of the most popular of the many songs written or translated by Walsh who was born in Derry in 1805 (he left the city while still very young). He was an influential and pioneer translator of Irish folk poetry. His work was widely known during the 1830s and '40s, being published, for example, in John O'Daly's *Reliquies of Irish Jacobite Poetry* (1844). A teacher by profession he was dismissed from his post on account of his connection with the *Nation*. Following this, he taught for a time at the convict school on Spike Island, only again to be dismissed for his action in saying a public farewell to John Mitchel on the occasion of his deportation. Walsh died in the Cork Workhouse in 1850.

As we proceed up the steep, tree-lined Shipquay Street our journey is near completion as we approach the heart of the city. St Columba, who is credited with founding Derry early in the sixth century, is credited also with a number of poems, some of which tell of his love of the place.

> Were all the tribute of Alba mine,
> From its centre to its border,
> I would prefer the site of one house
> In the middle of fair Derry.
>
> The reason I love Derry is,
> For its quietness, for its purity,
> And for its crowds of white angels
> From the one end to the other.
>
> The reason I love Derry is
> For its quietness, for its purity
> Crowded full of heaven's angels
> Is every leaf of the oaks of Derry.
>
> My Derry, my little oak grove,
> My dwelling and my little cell;
> O eternal God, in heaven above
> Woe be to him who violates it.

St Columba's contribution to literature extends far beyond the poems attributed to him. At least it is so held in popular myth where it is handed down that when he attended the convention of Druim Ceatt, which was held in the last decade of the sixth century, he did a great service to the poets of Ireland. This important gathering, convened principally to discuss political matters, took place on the Mullach, a grassy mound today better known as Daisy Hill and situated near Limavady. The site can still be seen (about a mile south west of the town, in Roepark Demesne, on the edge of what is now a golf-course) and it was here that Columba championed the cause of the *filid* or Gaelic poets. The poets had grown proud, overbearing and excessive in their demands for payments for their services. As a result, there was now an agitation for them to be expelled from Ireland. Robert Farren, in his remarkable long poem, *The First Exile* (1944), which is devoted to the life of Colmcille, has this to say:

The whole land was loud with the pounding of argument,
Out of a pit of a purple-black mountain
poets careered to confer and debate
what was left to be done before power put them hobbling
forever from Ireland in wreck and disgrace.
'Has the whole of the isle not a prince that loves poetry?'
Dallan squealed out like a boar among dogs;
and a Derryman's lips shot apart – but joy smothered him,
and he croaked without wit like a puddle of frogs.

'God', he said, 'God himself, the High Spirit Most Holy,
dipped into my mind and brought up the good memory
of one prince of Ireland in love with good poetry -
'tis Colm of Derry, and what king shall better him?'

'Colm out of Derry!',
'Ah, Colm!'
'A prince and apostle!'
'And a poet! Remember the song against fire for Derry!'
'And the exile-song, mournful as a wood-pigeon's, made
by Foyle-water.'

Eventually, Colm arrives to defend, 'the places and deeds and times of poets' and to defend, 'poetry herself' by striking the 'white-bronze gong of Righteous Dealing'. Farren's poem, and the old story that precedes his book, claims that Columba spoke so eloquently in the poets' defence that they were reprieved. The story has it that the twelve hundred poets who were present at Druim Ceatt rose to their feet in spontaneous appreciation of the saint's verbal potency.

Things do not change: language is important still, and poets in Ireland are numerous still; and still they are to be found in the thick of controversy.

And things do not change in Derry. Columba championed the poets, and for a time at least secured their prosperous and favoured place in Irish society; and he prized and praised the place of Derry. Centuries later O'Faolain, with all of his writer's instinct, championed Derry (the place the poet in Columba loved) as a place favourable to the social imagination of the modern novelist. The city has tugged at the imagination and fed the emotions of many, often with exciting creative results. One directly responsive example is Eona Kathleen MacNichol's historical and poetic novel (it is set in A.D. 563) *Colum of Derry* (1954).

In addition to the books, plays and poems mentioned already one must note some of the many occasional works produced by local people. These include I.F. Galwey's, *Hybrasil, and other verses* (1872) or Lily Marcus's, *War Poems* and the later *Lyrical Links* (1920) or Isaac Wilson's, *Poems for Pastime* (1967). In addition to these, the city has ties to works of wider significance and that are set in or are influenced by some aspect of the city.

Among these are Denis Johnston's 1937 radio drama *Lillibulero*; John Montague's, *The New Siege* (1970); Brian Friel's *Freedom of the City* (1973); Francis Stuart's *Memorial* (1973); Jennifer Johnston's *Shadows on our Skin* (1977); Thomas Kinsella's *Butcher's Dozen* (in the 1979 volume *Fifteen Dead*) and Frank McGuinness's *Carthaginians* (1988).

Things do not change. Frank McGuinness's play is set on the side of the same green hill that we believe Mrs Alexander looked out upon as she composed her hymn. The little hills of Derry that inspired Ledwidge still shelter the Foyle; the river that saw the leavetaking of so many, nurses and nurtures the city; the city is securely girt by its walls; the oak leaves on St Columb's green hills remains lush and numerous.

And, finally, we pass once more through the Diamond on our way back to New Gate and from there to the place where we began our journey. You may fancy, as you enter the very heart of the old city, that the air is full of half-realised images and shades – the forms of scribes and monks and poets, the smell of newly-crushed, still-wet ink, drying off the vellum, wafting out from the open door of the city's ancient mediaeval scriptorium; the golden evening light enlivened as it passes through the reds and the greens and the yellows of the Scriveners' stained glass window. You may see, if you wish, set out in gossamer stuff, the forms of those strolling players and preachers and printers and booksellers congregating under the angel-heavy trees in the Diamond; women and men, philosophers and writers, adventurers and dreamers, hymn-makers and rope dancers: all passing under the placid shadow of the ancient Town House and Exchange as it overlays the memorial to those who served and to the honoured dead of two world wars.

And, complimenting all of this complexity and richness, beside a bridge, two hands reach out; they touch, almost. About them, and about us, O'Faolain's words hang pregnant in the air. These words, springing from a belief in the power of the imagination and of the efficacy of the creative word, offer up, for those who wish to receive their message, a clear articulation of hope and of unity of purpose among the voices of the living and of the dead, a testimony to those who have imagined, created and made, and who continue (and who will continue) to enhance life by so doing.

II

Sunlight Falling Across Annish

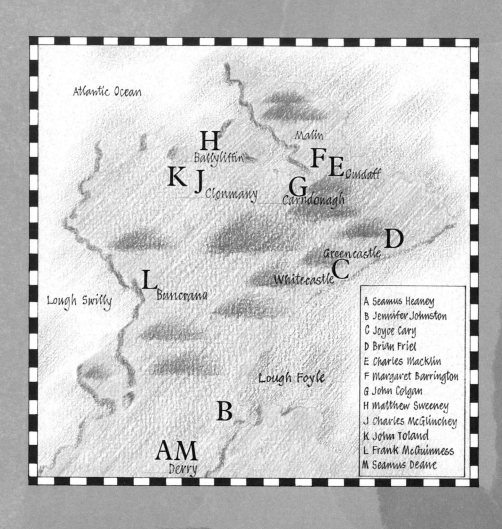

Sunlight Falling Across Annish:
Some Writers of Derry and Inishowen

Bridget O'Toole

This journey takes in the most northerly part of the island of Ireland, and one of the most romantic parts of Donegal; starting off from Derry, Bridget O'Toole completes a circular tour of Inishowen, that peninsula of green sward and grey stone cushioned between the waters of the Foyle and the Swilly. What she finds on her journey stimulates her to discuss the work of a group of writers who have two things in common – firstly, their indebtedness to people and to place and their connection to this one small corner of Ireland; and, secondly, their acknowledged stature as writers and the significance of their contribution to serious imaginative and creative literature. The writers include, among others, Seamus Heaney, Seamus Deane, Jennifer Johnston, Matthew Sweeney, Joyce Cary, Brian Friel and Frank McGuinness.

I decided to start off from Bishop Street, just outside the walls of the city and at the point where St Columb's College looks down onto the Bogside and across to Creggan. With its granity grey stone and its air of authority, it seems from below to merge with the city walls. Generations have come to it, some from the streets below, and within its stone walls have learnt the subtle lessons of conformity and subversion.

Past pupils include Brian Friel, Seamus Heaney and Seamus Deane, who have all become eminent in the literary world. Their work will be talked of on our journey from Derry round the Inishowen peninsula in Donegal and back again.

Seamus Heaney dedicates his poem, 'The Ministry of Fear' to his friend Seamus Deane who was a contemporary at St Columb's. In the poem, the two poets exchange verses against a background of authority, that of the school and that of the state. Heaney's resistance is in a refusal to declare part of his name on demand. The refusal is a significant one. He won't give his Christian name to the priest at school or his surname to the soldier at a road block.

these are the sort of directions you might be given to get to Whitecastle, which doesn't have a place sign on the road. It's best to think of it as a mile and a half beyond Quigley's Point. After the farm at the dip in the road you look down to the shore of the lough and there is a handsome white house. It was in the hands of the Cary family for generations, as was Redcastle a few miles further on and Castle Cary which was set against the mountain, *Cnoc a' Noinín* and is now no more. Whitecastle is on the shore and Castle Cary is against the mountain; Cary amalgamated them in his novel *Castle Corner* (1935). It is set in the 1880s and after, and in the most personal and specific way shows understanding of questions of land, emigration and exile. There are some lovely brief flashes of description of this part of Inishowen (which he calls Annish): 'A broad band of sunlight fell across Annish itself and suddenly the whole dark wet mountain sparkled almost to the top with cottage walls, white glittering points to the edge of the clouds.'

Just as Yeats, living in London, once saw a fountain in a shop window and was carried back by the sound to the Lake Isle of Innisfree, so Cary once had a glimpse of what took him back to Inishowen. This is how *A House of Children* (1951) begins: 'The other day, in an inland town, I saw through an open window, a branch of fuchsia waving stiffly up and down in the breeze; and at once I smelt the breeze salty, and had a picture of a bright curtain flapping inwards, and beyond the curtain, dazzling sunlight on miles of crinkling water'.

This enchanting combination of water and fuchsia is with us now as we drive between Whitecastle and Redcastle. Here the blossom-laden hedges almost touch the shore that skirts the road we are travelling on.

Cary's love for the place includes its inhabitants. He mocks the Irish, but no more exuberantly than he mocks the 'ascendancy'. His gifts as a novelist include a matter-of-fact sympathy for widely ranging characters. His women are particularly well-drawn.

The critic, Walter Allen, who taught for a while at the New University of Ulster (which is at Coleraine, directly across the lough) has written of Cary, 'more than any other writer of our time, English or American, he is the novelist of the creative imagination, for the creative imagination is the quality he most admires in human beings'. A painting on the door at Whitecastle, executed by one of Cary's aunts, shows figures from mythology. They are recognisable as Pan or Andromeda to those familiar with the classics but were interpreted differently by local people who saw in Andromeda a young woman from those parts who, it was said, had been seduced by Cary's father. So in Cary's novels, the grand themes are accessible as everyday realism.

He has a lightly worn omniscience and a moral sense which gives coherence but doesn't nudge the reader. In all his work, including *The Horse's Mouth, Herself Surprised* and *Mr Johnson*, he communicates tremendous enjoyment – he loves telling us about these people. He had, for the novelist, the happy combination of living a secure childhood, much of it in this place which was magical, and being aware of social uncertainties around him. He believed in the primacy of art and at the end of *The Horse's Mouth* gives us the powerfully positive image of a painter creating on a wall, even though he knows it is soon to be demolished.

The image might have some resonance for Brian Friel. He too conveys a disturbing sense of what is both undeniable and fragile in art. His is a very different perspective on Irish society. After Redcastle we must drive through Moville which looks, as we approach, like a little Mediterranean town on the curve of a bay. Moville was once the port for emigrant ships. It's now mainly a market town and holiday resort with tall elegant houses looking over the lough. We drive through its wide main street, still travelling north. From the short road to Greencastle we can see across the lough to the Mussenden Temple in Downhill (built as a library by the Earl Bishop of Derry and completed in 1785, the temple, which has a magnificent cliff top situation, was at one timed lined with books). Behind the temple we can see as far as Portstewart and Portrush and the entrance to the River Bann. The lough is now meeting the Atlantic as we approach the major fishing village of Greencastle where Friel lives. The boats lie close together in the little harbour which at times seems barely able to contain them. They are well built and cared for and have that smell of fish and diesel oil that is redolent of long arduous passages. They are painted with S O for Sligo, their port of registration, and have names like *Ard Mhuire, Provider, Random Harvester, Je Reviens...*

The area has various literary associations: Cary's family had holidays at a house near here called Carrigknock, as did the poet James Simmons who has written on Cary. Greencastle was the last home of D.J. O'Sullivan, naturalist, lighthouse-keeper, poet. In 1993, the year before he died, Lapwing Publications in Belfast brought out his poems *From Fastnet to Inishtrahull*, with an introduction by John Montague.

You would know that he lived most of his life surrounded by water because he writes less about the sea itself than what it brings him – flotsam, sea-birds, ships passing. His tender observations of the natural world are accurate and vivid. He communicates vast, generous pleasure in such creatures as crab, ladybird and oystercatcher with a brevity reminiscent of the imagists, or of early Irish lyric poetry. He is especially good on spiders, verbally enticing us into their journeys. The final poem in the volume, 'Memories' is pared right down to its final radiant image:

> Having lived in a lighthouse
> On a bare rock
> Surrounded by sea
> For most of my life
> And now retired.

The thing I remember
Is dense fog clearing
At the turn of high tide
And the stars coming out
Like primroses in the sky.

Brian Friel's house is down near the shore. He writes, however, of a different Donegal. Ballybeg, the fictional setting of many of his plays is not a place of fine residences, large vessels and open vistas. It is a small village set in rocky fields, closed in by the pressures of church, family and poverty. Friel is a great craftsman of the theatre. We sense the claustrophobia, mentally we understand the despair but, as audience, we are entertained. We even hope. He frequently lets us know early on what the fate of the characters will be; then he draws us into their lives and illusions by the power of his language and by the energy of his people. Only we never quite forget the disastrous outcome and this gives us that cohabiting of realism with optimism which feels true to Irish rural life. Actual disaster is never presented on stage but the knowledge of it lurks in a way that seems familiar in a place where people still preface plans with the phrase, 'if we're spared...'.

Philadelphia Here I Come (1965), *Translations* (1981) and *Dancing at Lughnasa* (1990) are among those works set in Ballybeg. His translation of Chekhov's *Three Sisters* (1981) though located in provincial Russia, could as easily have been near Ballybeg with its combination of exuberance and paralysis.

Friel lived and worked in Derry for some years and one of his best plays is *The Freedom of the City* (1974). Carefully set in 1970 it nevertheless satirises the response of the British state to the events of Bloody Sunday in 1972. Three working class Derry people, two men and a woman, find themselves accidentally occupying the Guildhall. It is both funny and tense and says sharp things about class, education, British-Irish relations and the uses and abuses of language, subjects which are not confined to Derry in the early 1970s.

Brian Friel is very much a professional man of the theatre, though he turns away from publicity and is said to include at least one deliberate inaccuracy in every biographical programme note. This would be in keeping with the notion of the irrelevance of accuracy to truth which comes across in many of his plays, especially *Faith Healer* (1980). It is, however, an ascertainable fact that he was a founder member of the Field Day Theatre Company (he resigned in 1994) which mounted plays by Irish writers and usually launched them in Derry. It has also published plays, poems, pamphlets, translations and, recently, *The Field Day Anthology of Irish Writing*. Heaney and Deane are both directors and Frank McGuinness has done work for them. The literary and theatrical camaraderie of the area reaches across the centuries: Friel has adapted a play by the eighteenth century Culdaff writer, Charles Macklin.

Culdaff is to the north west and we take a road that runs parallel to the coast though not always close to it. The sea is on our right and to the left lie acres of bog-land; locally, this is called 'the moss' in those parts where turf is cut. Grass and heather grow on it and different mosses of delicate green intricacy, but the predominant colours are pale rusty brown and black. Black is where the turf has been worked, leaving small cliffs with pools of water below. The turf are put up in rows to dry in the wind then built into stacks to wait before being hauled home. In fine dry weather we'll see many loads of turf travelling home, some spade-cut, in straight-sided blocks, but more and more likely these days to have been cut by machine. In the bars of Gleneely and Culdaff the debate and chat on the relative merits of spade or machine cut turf will pass the hours without urgency or acrimony.

There are different kinds and paces of traffic on these roads. Tractors pull not only turf or a few sheep in the trailer but may be used to go to the Post Office, to the shop or to Mass. In the prints left by their large wheels lie the blossoms in the year's succession, golden whins, white and pink may, the fallen red jewels of fuchsia. We may pass the occasional slow bicycle, its dark-clothed rider carrying a string bag. And we too may be passed and at speed, not by a Mr Toad in his latest shiny sports car, but by one of the cars of Inishowen, an Opel Kadett, holed and rusty, string trailing, tearing homewards.

Culdaff looks every inch the plantation village with its neat architecture and the one-and two-storey houses built round a triangle of green. The Church of Ireland edifice stands in the heart of it, slender and self contained. Its history reflects a pattern repeated in this part of Ulster. After land and church was confiscated from the Catholics in the early seventeenth century the rectors spent the next two centuries trying to acquire a congregation. Successful plantation resulted in a number of Protestant families settling here; many of them have since intermarried. A fascinating, detailed history of this parish and its different denominations is contained in Brian Bonner's *Our Inis Eoghan Heritage* (1972).

Charles Macklin is commemorated on a plaque on the green, just to our right as we enter the village. He was born near here in 1699, a Catholic, baptised Cathal MacLochlainn. The family left the village to live near Dublin when he was a child and as a young man he moved to England and began a career in the theatre. He became a Protestant, worked hard at acquiring an English accent and changed his name to Charles Macklin. From his early years he would have learnt where the power lay in the world, not only locally in Culdaff but from the experience of his father who had fought on the losing side at the Battle of the Boyne.

Macklin was a dedicated actor. He employed a 'method'-like saturation and research into each part and combined this with the energy of a powerfully forceful personality. The story goes that Pope said of his Shylock, 'This is the Jew / That Shakespeare drew'.

He wrote plays that contained the same wit and vigour that showed through in his acting. They include *Love á la Mode* (1759), *The True Born Irishman* (1763) and *The Man of the World* (1764).

Brian Friel's adaptation is of *The True Born Irishman* which he calls *The London Vertigo* (1990). It's a shortened version, very entertaining, fast-moving and humorous, exploring the possibilities offered by social pretentiousness meeting its downfall. Comic effects also result from the clash of two cultures – English and Irish – and stock theatrical devices like disguise and surprise. Friel calls his work on it 'a kind of *comhar* or cooperation or companionship with a neighbouring playwright'.

What is not evident from Friel's adaptation is that O'Dougherty, the hero of *The True-born Irishman* has a resounding pride in his nationality. Irritated beyond endurance by the affectations of his anglophile wife, who calls herself Mrs Diggerty, he evokes with passion the great names of his country.

> Ogh, that's right, Nancy – O'Dougherty forever – O'Dougherty! – there's a sound for you - why they have not such a name in all England as O'Dougherty – nor as any of our fine sounding Milesian names – what are your Jones and your Stones, your Rice and your Price, your Heads and your Foots, and Hands, and your Wills, and Hills and Mills, and Sands, and a parcel of little pimping names that a man would not pick out of the street, compared to the O'Donovans, O'Callaghans, O'Sullivans, O'Brallaghans, O'Shaghnesses, O'Flahertys, O'Gallaghers, and O'Doughertys – Ogh, they have courage in the very sound of them, for they come out of the mouth like a storm; and are as old and as stout as the oak at the bottom of the bog of Allen, which was there before the flood and though they have been dispossessed by upstarts and foreigners, buddoughs and sassanoughs, yet I hope they will flourish in the Island of Saints, while grass grows or water runs.

Culdaff now has a Charles Macklin Autumn School which enlivens the darkening days of October with a weekend of talks, workshops and readings.

Macklin's life was flamboyant, public and worldly. The next writer we shall meet, John Colgan of Carndonagh, led the life of a monk, dedicating his life to recording in Latin the lives and works of the Irish saints.

To find the road to Carndonagh from Culdaff we set out northwards in the direction of Malin town. For a few miles we are elevated above the land on either side. The road wasn't built that way but the ground on either side has sunk after the work of generations of turf cutters. Now grown over with grass and bog cotton it still shows black where the soil is broken. We pass whitewashed single-storey houses, lime splashed on to the flowers growing in the yard. Sometimes there will be an abandoned dwelling with grass growing deep into the thatch. In the rain few sights are more desolate and only the most confirmed sentimentalist could bewail its replacement by a modern bungalow whose large windows bring into the house light, sky and mountains. As we take a road west towards Carndonagh (known locally as 'Carn') the mountains are in front of us, a line of them making towards the sea like horses. Slieve Snacht is often solid white with snow in the winter when its neighbours are still ginger brown and there's Trawbreaga taking its name from Trawbreaga Bay, the 'treacherous strand'.

We come to a T-junction at the neck of this bay and if we look right we can see to the north the dunes at Five Finger Strand. Malin town is that way and beyond that, Malin Head. Growing up in Cornwall, I was enchanted by the names of the weather stations on the shipping forecast and later found their music in a poem of Seamus Heaney's.

> Dogger, Rockall, Malin, Irish Sea:
> Green, swift upsurges, North Atlantic Flux
> Conjured by that strong gale-warning voice
> Collapse into a sibilant penumbra,
> Midnight and close down.

Malin was the childhood home of Margaret Barrington whose novel, *My Cousin Justin* was reissued by The Blackstaff Press in 1990. Originally published in 1939, it came at the end of the decade which for Barrington included work in London at the BBC and for the left-wing paper *Tribune* and active support for the republican side in the Spanish Civil War. For a while she was married to the novelist and short-story writer, Liam O'Flaherty. *My Cousin Justin* was published in 1939, between Joyce Cary's *Castle Corner* (1938) and *A House of Children* (1941). Set further north in Inishowen it shares some of Cary's subject-matter: the complex relations between Anglo-Irish property owners and the local Irish and the intensity of feeling these people develop for the place where they grew up. If she lacks Cary's grace and flair, Barrington writes with vigour and intellectual clarity. There is a keen scrutiny of the political questions of the day; the characters are affected by the Home Rule debate, the Great War and the Irish Civil War. What is not openly examined as an issue, though it comes across clearly, is the struggle of a woman to be free of the domination of two overpowering men.

Socially isolated as they are, the narrator and her cousin have a more than ordinary allegiance to each other and to the terrain of north east Donegal. In the novel, Barrington scrambles the topography a little but this is recognisably Inishowen.

> Ten miles out of Derry we left the main road. Here the aspect
> of the country changed at once and instead of pleasant farm
> lands a wild, desolate and barren landscape stretched out

before us. Not so far as the eye could reach could be seen the white-washed walls of an isolated farmhouse, the smoke rising from a chimney. For miles on each side of the road the bog had been cut away so that it ran, a rough track, high over the surrounding country. Snow lay thick in the hollows and the bog-holes were frozen. Here and there small turf-stacks, left from the previous summer's cutting, showed like primitive dwellings, snow outlined the cracks on the windward side. On the far side of the bog the mountains rose, black against the wintry sky. A harsh wind blew from Scotland, cold and bitter, singing its whining song through the telegraph wires and whistling round the car. A land of Ossianic grandeur, cursed by a baleful eye.

Malin Town, as it is known locally, is really only the size of a village. It is uncannily neat and pretty; a well-shaven green is surrounded by tidy buildings, including the Church of Ireland church. It has won prizes for 'best-kept town'. There are seats and pleasant trees and a slightly menacing stillness. Some of the tensions which contributed to the civil war persist. The Big House, Malin Hall, is now owned by a Catholic; in their attitude to new neighbours, Protestant farmers are friendly, kind and wary.

The sort of political activity and international perspectives embraced by Margaret Barrington are not a reaction against the concerns of the parish. They are a liberation, a clarification of ideas which the facades of Malin's Diamond could nurture but never release.

Back at the T-junction, to reach Carndonagh, we take the left. On your approach, the first thing you see is the Church of the Sacred Heart floating, as it were, high over the town. There's something rather theatrical about the way its been positioned making Carn look from a distance like a French cathedral town. Once you arrive the church disappears and you find yourself in a typical small Irish market town. You have to have special antennae to park here. Tractors, vans and cars place themselves in The Diamond in a way that manages to be both haphazard and civilised. Double parking is the norm.

One piece of evidence of the existence of the writer we have come seeking is easily found: one of the town's largest buildings is the handsome 'Colgan Hall'. However, many details of his life still match the obscurity in which Colgan lived. He was probably born in 1592 in the townland of Priesttown which is now absorbed into Carndonagh. He may have been the John MacColgan who was a student in Glasgow around 1610, a skilled lawyer who spoke Irish and Latin. He left Ireland for good at the age of nineteen and was ordained about seven years later. He joined the Franciscans at Louvain and spent most of the rest of his life there working on the Irish manuscripts which were to become the *Acta Sanctorum*.

Louvain was a great centre of learning. The monks undertook projects on Irish history and culture, not only on the lives of the saints but also on the place names of Ireland, its antiquities, its kings and the main historical events of Ireland and Scotland. The lives of the saints were to be translated into Latin to make them accessible to all Europe.

Manuscripts came from throughout Ireland and so, for a while, did cash. However the upheavals of the time affected Irish monastic life and it became impossible to raise money. The arrival of Cromwell was only one indication that the old era had passed. Colgan did manage to complete one volume of the *Lives of the Irish Saints* in 1645 and, in 1647, the lives of Saints Patrick, Brigid and Colmcille.

He was said to have written in order to restore 'the neglected honour of his race and country'. He always denied credit for his work. Reading of his activities and those of the other monks who collected manuscripts, raised money and toiled away at translations and commentaries, it is impossible not to be impressed by the sense of how unimportant was individual fame in their great undertakings. I wonder how Colgan, who during his own lifetime worked away in sickness and poverty, would react to the idea put forward at a County Council meeting that money from the 1992 lottery should be allocated towards erecting his memorial. (I also wonder how Brian Friel reacted to the proposal at the same meeting that he should 'pen a play' on the life and times of John Colgan.)

Passing the Priesttown area (it was once called Muff, which adds some confusion), we take the road to Buncrana by way of Ballyliffin and Clonmany and if we glance back at the town its traffic idiosyncrasies are forgotten and once again the massive granite church is dominant. Between Carndonagh and Ballyliffin we pass where Trawbreaga Bay doesn't quite make it round the Isle of Doagh to create – or recreate – an island.

Ballyliffin is a small village with two very large hotels. The poet Matthew Sweeney was born here. He now lives in London (and has lived on the continent) and his poetry has a cosmopolitan range but he shares with other Irish poets a modest self-mockery as though he is afraid of seeming too set apart by his education and travels. Many of his poems are about lonely people, isolated dwellers in rented apartments; for instance, an old man caring for his invalid wife, or a German hitchhiker who has travelled 'Here to the apex of Ireland / where he can't get a lift'.

Connected with his own isolation is a feeling for the absurd which can throw up some surreal, disturbing images. For all he celebrates oddness he also creates a strong sense of warm friendships, humour and companionship. Several poems invite us to share jokes and good times. Pollan Bay is just to the north of here and Sweeney's poem of that name recreates the time he and a friend carried lobsters up from the shore in a baby bath of sea water. The poem which best evokes this region and which typifies his unblinking

compassion for the lonely and odd is 'Two Sisters ' from his 1983 volume
The Round House.

> One says there is nothing beyond the sea
> and behind the hills are imagined countries.
> She stands in the yard, stooped like a tree
> that the wind has pummelled these fifty years.
> A strand of hair covers her beak face.
> She thinks how the farm is eroded
> From full byres of cattle to a lease
> of all the fields, enforced by infirmity.
>
> On these, her rare steps outdoors
> she recalls the taste of spring water
> the morning hunts for new eggs in straw
> the potato diggings, the bringing of cans of tea.
> Indoors, shoving turf in an iron range,
> her sister keeps her English accent.
> Years ago she shut the door on the city.
> Her eyes are dim, the terraced houses fading.

The Clonmany area has been described as it was a hundred years ago in a book of reminiscences, *The Last of the Name* by Charles McGlinchey. McGlinchey, a weaver, recounted his memories to a schoolmaster, Patrick Kavanagh, in the 1940s and '50s. Kavanagh wrote them down and the resulting manuscript has in turn been edited and given an introduction by Brian Friel. As Friel points out, McGlinchey's life spanned Home Rule, the land wars, Parnell, the Easter Rising and two world wars. These things are not mentioned. Instead, we learn about emigration and what it really meant to work in Scotland for next to nothing on an empty stomach and of the man who was so seasick on the boat to America that only because 'some Malin men interfered' was he saved from being thrown overboard. He survived to prosper in Philadelphia and eventually to own a street of houses. We are told too of Jimmy Doherty's Latin School and how he taught his pupils while they walked along beside him as he set potatoes. There is nothing vague or rambling about these recollections, they are powerfully clear-cut and their accuracy is confirmed against wider historical events.

The book confirms the existence not only of an abundant Irish speaking culture but also of the classical knowledge celebrated by Friel in *Translations*, the play in which a life of learning flourished in Ballybeg to be threatened by the different kind of knowledge brought by the map-makers of the British army.

As we approach Clonmany the mountains seem to crowd near and round it. Perhaps this contributes to its feeling of isolation. Of all the places on our journey it seems to me to be the most remote from 'civilisation' and yet it has venerable associations. There are ancient crosses and standing stones all over Inishowen but here they are to be found in abundance. It was perhaps this, together with the pious reputation of John Colgan, who had died twelve years before he was born, that drove John Toland of the parish of Clonmany to a very different philosophical career.

Toland, born in 1670, was one of the most controversial thinkers of the enlightenment. It was of him that the term, 'freethinker' was first used and he is said to have coined the word 'pantheist' to describe himself. He was brought up a Catholic and an Irish speaker, but became a Protestant in his early teens. This was probably less from the careerist motives of Charles Macklin (a couple of decades later) than out of true conviction. He railed against priests, seeing their role in religion as unnecessary.

Like Colgan he was educated in Glasgow. Toland also worked in Holland and lived in Oxford and London. He admired Locke and in 1696 published his most famous work, *Christianity not Mysterious*, in which he put forward views that were both rational and radical. His assertion was that Christianity was accessible to anyone but that clerics had obfuscated its meaning for simple people, 'the uncorrupted doctrines of Christianity are not above their reach or comprehension, but the gibberish of your divinity schools they understand not'.

It is hard to imagine this going down well in late seventeenth century Clonmany – or Dublin: not only did the Irish parliament twice order the book to be burned by the common hangman, but there was a rumour that its author was also to be burnt. This cut short Toland's homecoming visit to Ireland.

Back in England his writing included work on an Irish dictionary, a critical history of Celtic religion and learning (for which he drew on his knowledge of druidic sites round Clonmany), various political pamphlets and one of the first biographies of John Milton. He found Milton a particularly attractive subject, sharing his political radicalism and religious nonconformism.

The epitaph Toland wrote for himself included the words, 'He was an assertor of liberty, a lover of all sorts of learning, a speaker of Irish, but no man's follower or dependent'. He appears to have antagonised many of his peers both by his behaviour and by what he thought. Berkeley and Swift attacked him, but he was admired by Voltaire and his ideas influenced Diderot. Perhaps there would be a good case for a John Toland summer school!

After our detour round Ballyliffin and Clonmany we join the more direct route between Carn and Buncrana. It's a mountainous road, the wildest and most desolate of our journey. Frank McGuinness came this way to and from school in Carn when he was growing up in Buncrana. Since coming to live in Inishowen I've often thought of him travelling this road and wondered what he dreamed about as the landmarks became familiar, the lake with the island on it, the distant glimpse of the sea between mountains, the two great craggy peaks called the King and the Queen, so named because of their resemblance to the chess pieces. No doubt these natural forms made a deep impression, but McGuinness's work seems distinctly urban and social. We were friends when we taught together at the New University of Ulster; he used to direct some of us in plays, usually comedies by Wilde, Coward and Alan Ayckbourn although there were also productions of Lorca and Shakespeare. He had the gift of turning the most dedicated introvert into a manic party-goer. His humour draws on caricature exaggerated beyond all reason to the delight of friends or audience. At first, his wit seems entirely iconoclastic.

For example: a group of friends making a play is a central part of *The Carthaginians* (1988). Its setting in a Derry graveyard; its ritual grieving is seen as paradigmatic of the city's condition after Bloody Sunday. What the play does most successfully is to celebrate the resourcefulness and humour of the Derry working class, the affection that lies behind the endless slagging and, importantly, the resilience. This 'play within a play' is one of the funniest things in modern theatre. Its manic humour excites us, the audience, as it walks a tightrope teetering towards, but never quite falling into, utter madness. The gaiety of its central character Dido, Queen of Carthage, is surely redemptive.

All McGuinness's plays from *The Factory Girls* (1982) through *Observe the Sons of Ulster Marching towards the Somme* (1986) to *Breadman* (1990) are about working-class people. He assumes we will take for granted their energy, wit and appetite for ideas. In the play about Caravaggio, called *Innocence* (1987) the cardinal tells the painter he reminds people of unpleasant truths: 'The painter of the poor. Dirty feet, rags, patches, kneeling in homage to their Virgin Mary, another pauper, mother of their God'. But the painter himself feels reproached by his models: 'You put our like in the light. Put us back into darkness'.

Baglady (1988) is the monologue of a derelict who has been abused and mentally damaged, whose mind moves convincingly in and out of her suffering. It's a *tour de force* comparable in its desolation and monologue technique with Friel's *Faith Healer* which McGuinness admires, giving it as one of his early inspirations to write.

The economic life of Buncrana is dominated by the shirt factory. His mother and aunts worked in it and their assertiveness and gift for spirited repartee has caused him to say that he was 'reared by actresses'. Recently he has also stressed the importance of his relationship with his father, possibly an inspiration for the hero of *The Breadman*. Yet, no-one should get the impression that McGuinness is a sentimentalist. He is a truth-teller whose denial of illusion or sentimentality becomes part of the theatrical process.

On the road from Carndonagh we had our first sight of the sea. Buncrana is on Lough Swilly with mountains beyond; we look over to the next peninsula of Donegal. Derry is only 12 miles away again now. Like Moville,

Buncrana is a holiday resort for Derry people. One of its most striking buildings is a green tower once rented by Joyce Cary and his family.

On this first part of the journey from Buncrana to Derry we have Lough Swilly on our right with the mountains beyond. It seems more visually appealing than Lough Foyle, probably because the far shore is closer and individual houses are clearly defined, set in small fields of many shades of green. Later, as we come near Derry, the way is dominated by the ancient fort, the Grianan of Aileach, a hill with the circle at the top from which four counties can be seen. There is a description of an outing to this in Jennifer Johnston's *Shadows on our Skin*. An entirely different kind of fort completes our journey back to the city. Both the refortified checkpoint at the border on the way in to Derry, and Fort George at the end of the Buncrana Road, hide their up-to-date technology behind grey/green metal walls. Unlike the Culmore Road checkpoint this one does have a literary association. Sam Burnside's poem, 'Coshquin Checkpoint' (*Fortnight*, March 1992) is a meditation on the spot where a proxy bomb exploded killing six people. He is struck by the bright flowers of six wreaths laid at the roadside and on a profoundly pessimistic level by the more enduring items taken for granted, flags and banners and 'glaring gable walls':

> Our symbols mean everything
> and change nothing.

On the Buncrana Road we pass a new building established to house an enlarged St Columb's College. One of the College's past pupils, Seamus Deane, talks of the ground vanishing beneath his feet when he returns to Derry. Deane's poetry is complex and restrained. He is not seduced by language as a means of giving pleasurable sensations but he will catch and use its ambiguities. Even though it may not have aroused strong feelings immediately, the atmosphere of a poem of his will stay in the mind. We do not learn until the last two lines who it is that steps across in the cold water of 'Fording the River'. The poem effectively combines the enduring and the immediate. The images of the river-crossing, the loved person vanishing and returning and the father-son relationship are archetypal. More contingent, but convincing by their arbitrariness, are the particular details of stones and forest and the poet's action.

> I had bent
> To examine a strand of barbed wire
> Looping up from a buried fence
> When I heard you shout.

The arbitrary image becomes the centre of attention in 'History Lessons', where major events of past and present are linked in his mind with the figure of a boy running across the school grounds in winter.

He writes of bitterness and coldness in his poems about Derry. In 'Derry', 'The unemployment in our bones / Erupting in our hands in stones', and in 'A Schooling' he yokes the cold of the government school milk with the iron waters of the harbour where his father is laying cables. It's another poem whose uncluttered images endure in the mind.

As a poet, Deane's wit never becomes laughter and the final impression is of a certain intellectual austerity. His criticism on the other hand is more genial, prepared to take risks, and generous in its appreciations. In the cliché-ridden world of literary criticism it is a pleasure to read him for his careful erudition and wideawake vocabulary. He has drawn attention to the subtleties of Friel, to the 'secret story' beneath the naturalism on stage and has traced some of Heaney's complicated responses to opposing cultural influences. In the case of other northern poets, Montague and Mahon, he has analysed their isolation and how connected it is with their sense of history.

Our sense of history and culture can only be enriched by *The Field Day Anthology of Irish Writing* of which Deane was general editor, and which was published in Derry. It is a real treasury, not only of poetry, fiction and drama but also of polemic theology, criticism and political memoirs. Most of the writers mentioned in this itinerary are included. Some dark moments of history are there: Cromwell's account of the taking of Drogheda in Volume I and in Volume III Noel Browne's encounter with the Irish bishops when he was trying to introduce a free health service. Extracts from the work of Bernadette Devlin and Eamon McCann impress with their clarity and their urgency in combining ideas with action. No wonder poets and academics see a vigour and eloquence in political engagement! This is not the time to chronicle the complex debate between *Field Day* and its critics as to how healthy or even accurate its writers may have been in their definition and uses of nationalism. Were *Field Day's* politics, as shown in *Translations* and in some of the pamphlets, a backward-looking dream and a divisive one at that? Is it any longer useful to talk of 'the colonial power'? It may be that one of the more interesting offshoots of the debate they engendered will be the accuracy and imagination with which liberal northern Unionists begin to define their culture.

Heaney and Deane have both taught in America, and Heaney was recently Professor of Poetry at Oxford; in both places the cultural influences are strong and self-confident. How much, one wonders, has this contributed to an assertion of Irish identity which would, or might have been, less strongly expressed had they stayed at home?

There are too few women represented in the anthology. The poet Eavan Boland sees this as indicative of its conservative nationalism. It may be that, with no women among the editors or the directors of *Field Day*, no effort was made to disclose the ones 'hidden from history'.

The anthology is still a great achievement and to handle it after all the critical discussion is to be reassured of the enjoyment it guarantees. It may turn out to be *Field Day's* greatest achievement. In hindsight, there were obvious difficulties in running a theatre company for Derry when none of its directors lived in the town. The footnotes in the anthology are for a non-Irish audience, American, Canadian, Australian perhaps. *Field Day* has in *some* way compensated Derry for the siting of Northern Ireland's second university elsewhere.

This has been very much a journey through a landscape and we have not been inside any buildings. Would the fuchsia seen through an open window, or the Child of Prague in his red china robe, or views through the white lace curtains, or the television, or the turf stove, give us any more clue than the landscape as to why this part of Ireland should produce or harbour so many good writers? We would learn something by listening to the people – but that requires a longer journey, one for another day.

III

The Glow upon the Fringe of a Great Flame

The Principal Gaeltacht areas of County Donegal

The Glow upon the Fringe of a Great Flame: North West Ulster's Writers in Irish

Diarmaid Ó Doibhlin

Diarmaid Ó Doibhlin's westward travels lead him among remote townlands and through some spectacular landscapes ; here he recollects and rediscovers some of the north-west's many creative and imaginative writers who have worked in Irish. During his journey he identifies the four Gaeltacht areas he considers to be the most important creative centres for literature in Donegal; it is in these districts that he locates the still potent influence on the imagination of townland, community and language; he looks, too, at how the tradition continues to be enlivened and enriched by Donegal writers of the standing of Cathal Ó Searcaigh.

Although I started from the city of Derry I set off immediately towards Letterkenny along a splendid, broad road newly constructed with European moneys. I had chosen to begin my journey proper in Rathmullan because ironically it was in Rathmullan that it all came to an end. When on 14th September 1607 the Gaelic princes of the North, O'Donnell of Tír Chonaill, the great O'Neill of Tyrone and Maguire of Fermanagh, began their perilous journey into exile on the continent of Europe 'leaving their patrimonies for ever' they left behind an indigenous culture that now had to face a ruthless and efficient colonisation. Aindrias Mac Marcuis, bardic poet from Tirhugh, contemplated the whole affair in understandable gloom. Fifty years earlier Fearflatha Ó Gnímh, from County Antrim, had in verses of terse *deibhidhe*, described the impending ruin which he sensed all around him:

> Táirnig a ré, leath ar leath,
> Scol Uladh, éigse Laighneach
> Deachmhadh damh Muimhneach, ní mhair,
> Ár gan fhuighleach an t-ársin.

Piece by piece, it came to an end
The Ulster school, the Leinster bards,
The tribute to the Munster poets
Remained unpaid; so nothing was left.

The medieval world was dying on its feet, the hereditary learning would shortly be eclipsed and the whole indigenous culture would find itself in acute peril.

The sons of the learned families found their refuge in the Irish brigades, in the armies of France and Spain and in the Irish colleges which were springing up in European cities. Michael Ó Cléirigh from Kilbarron, came to St Anthony's College in Louvain and guided there by his colleague, Father Hugh Ward from Lettermacaward, began the business of 'sifting, winnowing, straining' to put together the *Annals of the Kingdom of Ireland*, a work which is sometimes called the *Annals of the Four Masters*, which in many respects is the great glory of Donegal.

At home in Ireland, the centre of literary activity in the north in the Gaelic world seems to have shifted away from Donegal and Fermanagh to the south-east of Ulster. This may have been due to the pressures of colonisation and the movement of peoples in those days of upheaval. Donegal at any rate, to a large extent, slips out of the literary scene.

There was, however, one notable exception, Séamus Ó Gallchóir, Bishop of Raphoe, published in 1736 a remarkable collection of sixteen sermons in Irish which remained very popular throughout the eighteenth and nineteenth centuries. Ó Gallchóir was a native of the diocese of Kilmore but his position in the Raphoe diocese would have required him to be active on the mission throughout most of Donegal. His collection of sermons was unusual in several ways. Although printing had been in vogue since the fifteenth century, the native Irish, apart from brief experiments in Louvain and Paris, had clung to the old tradition of the transmission of literature by manuscript. Ó Gallchóir, by having his sermons published in book form was to a certain degree in penal Ireland breaking new ground. There were at least ten editions of his book in the eighteenth century, and I have been told that old speakers of Donegal Irish at the turn of this century knew whole passages of Ó Gallchóir off by heart.

Ó Gallchóir's sermons are written in simple and direct style, and his metaphors and imagery are culled from the lives and experiences of ordinary people. While he almost certainly faced the most difficult and harrowing physical conditions, he was nevertheless able to draw on the experience of a highly developed register within the Irish tradition, the register of religious prose writing. Ó Gallchóir's contemporary and associate, Aindrias Ó Doinnshléibhe, published in 1742 a dual-language catechism in Irish and English. Both Ó Gallchóir and Ó Doinnshléibhe handled Irish with clarity and precision. I have on my desk a little green catechism which the Catholic clergy of Raphoe issued in 1948. Here again one finds a similar clarity and aptness of expression, the register of religious prose still highly cultivated. It is after all a tradition which stretches back through Ó Doinnshléibhe at Paris (he was prefect of studies at the Irish College there, and Ó Gallchóir had been a student there), and Ó hEodhasa at St Anthony's College in Louvain in 1611 and to the *Catechismus Maior* of Peter Canisius.

I mention all this here because only recently a distinguished French critic, Angela Renaldi, has reminded us again of the importance of religious prose in the overall development of prose forms in literature. Economically and socially the native tradition had become marginalised, with the natives pushed out to the mountainous areas and to the seaboard. Yet, in spite of this, certain registers continued to be cultivated, and the religious register was one of these.

In 1910 Íde Mac Néill from the Glens of Antrim in collaboration with Séamus Ó Searcaigh from Cruit published a small collection of tales entitled *Cú na gCleas*, which had been taken down in Rannafast. Most interestingly one of her informants was Séamus Ó Grianna who was later to emerge as one of the most prolific prose writers in Irish to come out of Donegal. The Mac Grianna tale in content and taste had many of the qualities of early epic, reaching back to the Red Branch knights at Emain Macha and to Cú Chulainn and all that world of great deeds and heroic figures. It is a quite remarkable survival and tells us a great deal about how tenaciously these marginalised Irish had clung to their memories and how skilful they were in transmitting them.

The song tradition, too, survived despite not a little clerical interference. One often wonders what the clerics who had presented that little green catechism I have mentioned would have made of these lines from 'Geaftaí Bhaile Bhuí' which Sean O'Boyle noted down in Rannafast in 1944:

> Bhí mé lag gan bhrí, gan mhisneach in mo chroí,
> is í agam ar mhín sléibhe
> Bhí an codladh do mo chloí is b'éigeán domhsa luí
> agus d'imigh sí ina fíormhaighdean.

> I was weak and purposeless, no courage in my heart
> When I had her on the hill-top;
> Sleep bore me down and I simply had to lie
> And she went away, still virgin.

There had ever been within the native tradition a balance and a space, and so one finds in eighteenth century manuscripts serious religious and moral materials, hymns to the Blessed Virgin and prayers, set down alongside burlesque materials and prose and verse pieces which the cataloguers not infrequently describe as 'indecent'.

The literary developments came with the founding of the Gaelic League in 1893. The league, which after a slow beginning, began to make its influence felt throughout the country, had two basic aims: the preservation of the living language in the country and the creation of a modern and effective literature in Irish. Philosophically, the Gaelic League was rooted in late western romanticism with its emphasis on the natural world, rural values and the celebration and cultivation of the past. The teachings of both Fichte and Herder were important, too, with their emphasis on clinging to the *Volksgeist*. The league saw to it that proper emphasis was placed on the living speech of the ordinary people and that the new literature was built on Gaeltacht Irish. It was to be expected that it was the Gaeltacht areas in Donegal that became the creative centres of the new literature and that in it there was much celebration of that Gaeltacht world and its perceived values.

There were in the early years of this century, four principal Gaeltacht districts in Donegal. Firstly, and most importantly, there is that part of the county we may call the Rosses and Gaoth Dobhair which embraces that stretch of country from the Gweebarra River, northwards to Dunfanaghy, indeed even as far East as Creeslough itself. Niall Mac Giolla Bhríde who wrote the well-known ballad 'The Hills of Donegal' also published in Irish an account of his own life. He had grown up outside Creeslough and gained a certain amount of fame in his time when he was persecuted by the authorities for having his name in Irish on his cart. Pádraig Mac Piarais defended him in the courts, and when the case was lost the affair became the subject of a highly humorous song 'An Trucailín Donn' still widely sung throughout the Donegal Gaeltacht.

The second Gaeltacht district includes Glenfin and runs, broadly speaking, from just outside Ballybofey to Glenties, northwards as far as the Gweebarra River and eastwards to Glenswilly. Thirdly, there is what I call the Glencolumcille district including the parish of Glencolumcille, Teelin, Kilcar and Carrick, and reaching out towards Killybegs. Finally there is the Fanad peninsula with Rosguill and Carrigart to the west and Uiris and Clonmany to the east on the opposite shore of Inishowen. This is a rough description of the principal Gaeltacht districts – a Gaeltacht which under modern economic and social pressure continues unfortunately to dwindle. Each of these districts played its role in the evolution story of the new literature.

In many ways the most important district in this respect is that of the Rosses and Gaoth Dobhair. Of principal interest here is Rannafast a small peninsula situated between Gweebarra and Gaoth Dobhair. The earliest inhabitants may have come there no earlier than the late eighteenth century but by the early years of this century this townland had become a mecca for language enthusiasts from all over the north of Ireland. Lorcán Ó Muireadhaigh opened his famous Coláiste Bhríde there in 1918 and it survives to this day. Ó Muireadhaigh and others had noted how strongly the oral tradition had survived there and appreciated the fluency and richness of the spoken Irish there. At the lower end of the townland – for Rannafast is really a townland – there lived the quite remarkably gifted Mac Grianna family. The father, Feilimí Dhónaill Proinsias, was by all accounts an excellent *seanchaí* with an ear for the precise turn of phrase, while the mother Máire Eibhlín was an O'Donnell and the possessor of a large repertoire of traditional songs. Her brother Johnny Shéimsín was a well-known storyteller, and a collection of tales taken down from him was published in book form in 1948. The family was related on the mother's side to a number of nineteenth-century folk poets in Rannafast.

Séamus Ó Grianna was the eldest boy in a family of eleven children and received his early education at the local national school. Like many of his contemporaries in Rannafast and elsewhere in the Gaeltacht, he was hired out as a young boy and spent at least one season in Scotland at harvest work. After a period of private study he entered for a King's scholarship award and was successful. He trained as a primary school teacher in St Patrick's Training College, Drumcondra, Dublin, and graduated in 1914. He was never comfortable as a teacher and he later transferred to the civil service. In 1912 he won his first Oireachtas literary prize, published his first novel in 1921, and from then until his death in 1969, published some twenty-six other books – short stories, novels and autobiographical works.

Pádraic Ó Conaire and Pádraig Mac Piarais had pioneered the short story form in Irish and Ó Grianna was a prolific writer in this genre. He inclined in his short stories to promote his own form of the genre by adapting aspects of the folktale. He often for example prefixes his stories with long-winded introductions not unusual in the folktale. His characterisation too tends not to afford any psychological development or growth and is directed towards the general rather than the particular. So it is that certain stereotypes appear and reappear in his vast collection of stories, and certain personal pieties occur again and again. He returns also time and time again to the theme of love in his stories and again this is the stereotyped love of the *amour courtois* which I presume came to him through his mother's repertoire of love songs. His best work in my view is to be found in *Nuair a bhí mé Óg* (1942) and *Saol Corrach* (1945) where there is an edge to his prose and a keenness of vision and perception. He was a master of irony and had an acerbic wit which he might have put to more profitable use in his work. In many ways he failed to achieve his full potential. Nevertheless it has to be said that he took a language that had seemed to be on the point of extinction and that he, more than any other writer, demonstrated its potential as a subtle and flexible literary tool.

His younger brother Seosamh was to a large extent exposed to similar influences but had a much more developed perception of his role as a literary artist. He had the avowed intention of using the speech of his people 'in another way'. His most successful work, *An Druma Mór*, was written in 1935 but, owing to lack of official concern or efficiency, remained in civil service archives unnoticed until 1969. It is set in Ros Cuain (Rannafast) and explores ultimately the conflicts that exist between the materialistic world we all inhabit and the imaginative life of the soul. There is throughout the book a subtle commentary on the psychological effects of the cultural shift from Irish to English, a development of which the author was acutely conscious. There are rich veins of humour running through the novel that lighten the conflicts around which the story develops. Mac Grianna's highly acclaimed autobiography *Mo Bhealach Féin* (1940) begins with a flourish but tends, in my view, to lose focus and to fall away. All his writings reveal a genuine self confidence in his own artistic gifts and there are frequent passages of sustained lyric beauty when he evokes the mountains and sea and spaces of his own Donegal. He was by conscious choice a literary artist. A note of his in an unpublished diary runs:

> Within me long ago
> A poet's soul was born
> A music and a glow
> Like the glow
> Dark upon the fringe
> Of a great flame.
> I saw the hidden
> Wealth of life.

He was in every sense of the word a romantic but in a work first published in *An tUltach* in 1924, when he was twenty-three years of age, he gave us 'Ar an Trá Fholamh', a short story which I believe to be as fine a piece of writing as has been done in modern Irish. It is a simple story from famine Ireland based on a memory which is recorded in his brother's book *Rann na Feirste*. Mac Grianna transforms the basic raw material – the death from starvation and subsequent burial of a brother – into a superbly harrowing tale about the survival of the human spirit. Set against the bleak and barren landscape of famine-stricken Ireland where death, despair and terror seep through a drab and grey land, there can only be light and hope where the human spirit continues to meet its human obligations.

Out of this townland too came two books by Eoghan Ó Dónaill, *Scéal Hiúdaí Sheáinín* (1940) and *Na Laethe a bhí* (1953); these are traditional accounts of Rannafast and Gaeltacht life based on personal memories in the last years of the nineteenth century and the early years of the twentieth century.

Niall Ó Dónaill from nearby Lochanure was a cousin of the Mac Grianna brothers and like them could call upon a huge reservoir of traditional Irish. His *Na Glúnta Rosannacha* (1952) is a splendid account of the story of the Rosses as it lived in men's minds and is redolent of the landscape and the folk traditions of the people. It is essential reading and demonstrates the power and the warmth of the living tradition. Ó Dónaill has written with a superb and unequalled lyricism.

The village of Annagaire which lies between Rannafast and Lochanure produced Tadhg Ó Rabhartaigh who spent many years as a schoolteacher in County Leitrim and whose most ambitious novel *Thiar i nGleann Ceo* (1953) dealt with the lives and affairs of the mining community on the Sligo/Leitrim border. Into this he has woven events from the War of Independence and a love story. The focus of the novel is consequently somewhat distorted. In nearby Leitir Catha Maghnus Ó Dónaill who wrote under the pen name of Fionn Mac Cumhaill was born. He wrote some ten books of stories, set in the main in the Rosses and evoking simple county life and rural attitudes and values. I still find his *Na Rosa Go Bráthach* (1939) a most enthralling read, despite weak characterisation and a meandering plot. He had a fine ear for the music and flow of traditional Irish and records it authentically.

Leaving Annagaire and following the coast road we come into the parish of Gweedore, which embraces a wide stretch of country reaching down towards Machaire Rabhartaigh and Doire Chonaire (which are in the parish of Cloughaneely). Gweedore surprisingly, in comparison with other smaller communities in and around it, has not produced a great deal of creative writing. While here we should note Seán Mac Fhionnlaoich who was a native of Gola, an island that lies off the coast. He lived in Gweedore having taught for a number of years in Dunlewy, Mín a Chladaigh and Bunbeg, where he ended his days. His *Is Glas na Cnoic* and *Scéal Ghaoth Dobhair*, and *Ó Rabharta Go Mallmhuir* are built around memories of his childhood days on the island, and have a strong awareness of community and the bonds that hold a community together. Péigí Rose is the pen name of Seán Ó Gallchóir who now lives in Cnoc Fola; he is a native of the Gweedore parish. He has published some short stories and some poems, and while his output is not, as yet, very extensive he has the potential to produce creative writing of a high quality. Few authors, in my experience, writing in Irish today have his ability to catch the texture and colour of place or moment with the fullness and accuracy that he frequently achieves.

Moving further along the coast we come to Gortahork in the parish of Cloughaneely – a parish which has produced a higher than average number of competent writers. Micí MacGabhann's *Rotha Mór an tSaoil* (1958) is possibly the best known book to come out of Cloughaneely Parish. MacGabhann's book was successfully translated into English by Valentin Iremonger in 1962 as *The Hard Road to Klondyke*. The book was autobiographical and was dictated by MacGabhann to his son-in-law, the internationally known folklorist, Seán Ó hEochaidh. These materials were then edited by Proinsias Ó Conluain. The book describes the experience of growing up in Doire Chonaire in the last half of the nineteenth century. MacGabhann did seasonal work in Scotland, before heading off for America where he took part in the gold rush. Having acquired some capital he returned to Bealtaine in Gortahork, where he ended his days. He had little formal education and yet he demonstrates in these pages an almost perfect control of the rhythms and music of native Donegal Irish and, without sentiment or the misty romanticism which tends often in Donegal writers to blur the vision, he paints a remarkable picture of life in this parish. He emerges as a tough, shrewd and balanced human being with a great well of humour in his make-up. MacGabhann's book is undoubtedly a classic.

From Gortahork too came Eoghan Ó Colm, who was for many years priest on Tory island and whose book on Tory, *Toraigh na dTonn* (1971) is an affectionate insight into the close-knit lives of people on the island. And, since we have mentioned Tory, we recall here Séamus Mac an Bhaird who was a native of the island and whose *Troid Bhaile an Droichid* (1907) charmed generations of school-goers in the twenties and thirties of this century and introduced them to the natural flow and thrust of native Donegal Irish in all its vigour.

Gortahork too is Cathal Ó Searcaigh's home district. Ó Searcaigh is a young contemporary poet of outstanding talent and promise. His first poems date from the early seventies and it is fair to claim that his work gave Donegal a prominent place in the quite remarkable flowering of poetry in the Irish language in the seventies and eighties. To my mind there is in his more recent work a maturity and self assurance and, most importantly, a vitality that marks him out as one of the leading poets in modern Ireland. To date he has published four volumes of verse and his work has been translated into German, Italian and Spanish. In 1993 he received the Seán Ó Ríordáin award for poetry. Máire Mhac An tSaoi has said of him 'he evokes the mystique of his Donegal with passion and gusto'. Ó Searcaigh is conscious of the powerful effect of the music of Donegal Irish and he draws on this more and more in his poems. Ó Searcaigh's sensibility to landscape ensures that places such as Mín a Leá, Caiseal na gCorr and Bealtaine will become familiar to many readers at home and abroad. And it is worth recalling here that Coláiste Uladh in Gortahork, founded in 1906, brought together in this parish such distinguished writers of Irish as Séamus Ó Grianna, Manus Ó Dónaill, (alias Fionn Mac Cumhaill) already mentioned and as professor among them, Séamus Ó Searcaigh, from Cruit, who had an established reputation both as a writer and as a scholar of Irish.

The second broad Gaeltacht area I have mentioned is the Glenfin district. Glenties itself was the native village of Séamus de Chreag (1861-1934), who made important contributions to the study of Irish grammar. His short novel *Iascaireacht Shéamuis Bhig* (1904) was widely used in northern schools in the twenties and thirties. At the other extremity of this district is Glenswilly, where Senator Peadar Mac Fhionnlaoich was born. He was a prolific writer of articles on historical topics. He also wrote short stories and was as well a keen revivalist of the Irish language. He wrote a number of plays, including *Eilís agus an bhean déirce* (1900) the first play in Irish ever produced.

Seán Mac Meanman was by far the most important writer to come from this district. He was born in Ceann Garbh in 1896 and before his death in 1962 had published fifteen books which are veritable storehouses of the rich dialect of the area. Mac Meanman saw himself essentially as a *seanchaí* recording the life and values of an earlier generation and he sought assiduously, through the recording of the life and folk beliefs and attitudes of ordinary Gaeltacht people, to reveal that hidden Ireland which 'had survived in the Gaeltacht. His work is valuable for the many glimpses he gives into the social life and practices of the Gaeltacht in the final years of the nineteenth century. His main concern seems to have been to record and transmit the dialect of the Irish that was the language of the people where he lived.

There had been in the nineteenth century in Glenfinn and Glenswilly small schools of folk-poetry, with such writers as Tadhg Ó Tiomanaí, Peadar Breathnach and Conall Mac Daíbhidh. The memory of them and their work was alive in Mac Meanman's time. Aindrias Ó Baoighill, also a native of this district, based a quite successful and straightforward novel *An Dílidhe* (1930) about the experiences of a young boy as he grows and comes to grips with the difficulties of life.

By far the strongest Gaeltacht area, however, in this district was the Cruacha Gorma or the Bluestack mountains where, in the glen between Stucán and Gaigín, Irish survived with amazing vigour and purity right down to our own time. It was here that Sean Ó hEochaidh made the vast collections of oral materials which are now housed with the Folklore Commission in Dublin and which will be published in due course. Áine Ní Dhíoraí's superb collection of folk materials from the Bluestacks *Na Cruacha: Scéalta agus Seanchas* (1985) gives an idea of the range and quality of this material.

The Gaeltacht of the Fanad district has produced its writers too. Bríd Ní Dhochartaigh was born here. She taught in Monaghan and her three short books were aimed specifically at learners of Irish. Pádraig Mac Giolla Cheara, too, was a native of Fanad. Unlike many of the writers I have mentioned he had considerable formal education and spent long years as parish priest of Cloughaneely where he is buried. He was a gifted writer and concentrated in his writings on ecclesiastical matters such as church history and moral theology. He also made available a very readable and free flowing translation of the New Testament which many northern clergy still prefer to use. His *Ceachta as Leabhar na Cruinne* (1940) is perhaps his most interesting work. In it he describes in the most minute detail the ebb and flow of the natural world around him. In all this he was extending the range of the Irish language and demonstrating the facility the language had for precision. By any standard he is a stylist of distinction and deserves rather more attention than has hitherto been accorded to him.

In south Donegal, in Teelin and Glencolumcille, we recall the poetic contributions of Pádraig Ó Beirn who was born in Malinbeg in 1857. He wrote a considerable corpus of verse which was published in newspapers in America. Heavily influenced by late romantic poetry in English, his verse is not unlike the poetic creations of Douglas Hyde and other contemporary revival poets. Séamus Ó Doraidhin from Kilcar wrote verse in a similar vein. Cruachlann in Teelin at the foot of Slieve Liag is the birthplace of Seán Ó hEochaidh, whose life work has been to collect for the Folklore Commission the folk tales, *seanchas* and traditions of the Gaeltacht in Donegal.

Many of these writers lived away from their native Gaeltacht areas. In Dublin, Seosamh Mac Grianna, in many senses the most gifted, the most imaginative of them all, was sitting alone late one night, putting the finishing touches to an old story from his childhood in Rannafast. At the very end he slipped in a passage which has nothing to do with the story he has just finished and which seems to have escaped the attention of the editors at the *Gúm*. It is really a note about himself, and it is Joycean in style. It shows that his mind is full of the hills of Donegal and of their loneliness and mystery, and how the oral tradition of his people with its wonders and hopes and prophecies still haunt his imagination and consciousness. It deserves to be quoted in full:

> Sin uilig é. Tá mé ag cur deireadh leis agus é domhain san oíche. Tá cuid cnoc Thír Chonaill os coinne m'intinne, iad féin agus a gcuid scálí agus a gcuid uaignis…Nach cuimhin leat len aithris mar tugadh an Ghlas Ghaibhleanna mhór go Toraigh ar lorg a rubaill? Marcach sí Bheinn Eibhne a bhíodh ag siúl le Ó Dónaill…idir speal agus corran a thiocfas an cogadh…Dún Cruitín, Dún Cruitín fá mbuailtear smitín…

> That's all. I end this, deep in the night. The hills of Donegal are in my mind, they and their shadows and their loneliness…don't you remember the way to tell how the Glas Ghaibhleanna [a magical cow] was brought over to Tory Island seeking her tail? The fairy horse-man of Beinn Eibhne who used accompany Ó Dónaill…(that) the war will come between the reaping hook and the scythe…Dún Cruitín, Dún Cruitín where some will be beaten…

Postscript

This has been a swift journey across Donegal and through time. Back now in Derry city the creative impulse here in the Irish language is still strongly evident. Cathal Ó Searcaigh is poet-in-residence at the University of Ulster and public readings of his poetry have attracted wide attention. Greagóir O Dúill, poet and critic, has come to live in Gort an Choirce and has held the position of writer-in-residence in the Verbal Arts Centre in London Street in Derry. Novelist Séamas MacAnnaidh works with BBC Radio Foyle. Radio Foyle, it must be said, is contributing positively and Anne Craig in *Meascra* has presented some imaginative and informative programmes, including some excellent plays for children by Dave Duggan, a writer living in Derry. Pádraig Ó Croiligh, whose *Ceantair Shamhalta* (1971) had considerable promise, is at present administrator in the parish of Steelstown where a growing all-Irish primary school augurs well for the future of Irish in the city. Dr Nollaig Mac Congail of University College, Galway is a native of Derry and has made some specialised studies of the literature of the Donegal Gaeltacht. Seán Ó Siadhail, Professor of Irish at the University of Halifax, in Canada, has recently carried off a major *Oireachtas* literary award for a new novel. Tomás Ó Canáinn, an expert in Irish traditional music, has published a biography of Seán Ó Ríordáin. Ó Siadhail and Ó Canáinn are both natives of Derry. The Central Library in Derry through the imaginative input of Críostóir Mag Fhearaigh has been hosting a continuing series of readings by creative writers and is thereby sustaining a small but eager and highly motivated audience.

And so the glow upon the fringe burns still, kept alive by local interest and invigorated by the winds blowing from the wider world. There is clear evidence that the next generation will transmit the tradition with confidence and creativity. I end my journey on an optimistic note.

> Good night I said and God be with
> The tellers of the tale and myth,
> For they are of the spirit stuff
> That rides with Count O Hanlon.

IV

Deep Rivers, Dry Houses

A Sam Burnside
  James Simmons
B John Dunlap
  William Gray
C Francis Allison
  James Porter
D Francis Harvey
  (see journey no 1)
E Seumas MacManus
  Ethna Carbery
F William Allingham
G Patrick MacGill
H Peadar O'Donnell
  Paddy The Cope
  (Gallagher)

Lough Swilly

Tory Island

Bloody Foreland

DERRY

Grianán of Ailigh   A

Meenmore   Letterkenny

H

Raphoe

Ballindrait
Straboane
C
B

Glenties   G

E Mountcharles   D Donegal

Killybegs

F Ballyshannon

Deep Rivers, Dry Houses:
Some Radical Writers from the North West

Cahal Dallat

Cahal Dallat undertook a journey from Derry city to the west coast of Donegal, breasting the Bluestack mountains before taking to the coast road and then back again by way of the beautiful Poisoned Glen. On the way he discovered some new writers and rediscovered others. In this account of his journey he ponders on the nature of landscape, place, geography and politics and on the relationship of these to those imaginative writers whose inner drive is to pierce to the root of community and social experience. During what is a journey of discovery he considers the poetry and prose of James Simmons, Patrick MacGill, Peadar O'Donnell and William Allingham, among others.

The isolation, and sometimes the desolation, that the term 'north west' conjures up are as evident in Galicia, Brittany, Cumbria as in Alaska and the 'North-West Passage' or Afghanistan and the 'North-West Frontier': since capital cities often tend towards the centre or south east, the opposite becomes a byword for rugged conditions. So, as the Lake District represented nature for English writers, and the Rockies and the Yukon of Jack London and Robert Service represent the final frontier for Americans, Donegal will always hold a fascination for Irish writers.

What is less often noticed is that 'northwests', dogged by climatic and geological harshness, and at the maximum displacement from lush agriculture and cushy jobs, often become a focus for political activity, separatist, as in Brittany, or reformist as in Manchester, with the work of Robert Owen and Engels. Robert Tressell, too, who wrote *The Ragged-Trousered Philanthropists* (1914), a seminal novel about the exploitation of workers, came from the north west of England. But the region's role in the British labour movement was very much due to its vast numbers of Irish immigrants: Engels' views were certainly influenced by Mary and Lizzie Burns; Eva Gore-Booth, who worked as a socialist and feminist in

Manchester, dreaming, as Yeats wrote, 'some vague Utopia', had her political conscience formed in Sligo, (she is recalled in Lissadell Street in Salford); and even Tressell – whose real name was Noonan and whose father was an R.I.C. Inspector from the north west of Ireland – owed his painfully acute awareness to the combination of education and family origins.

Joyce has the 'Home Rule sun rising up in the north west', and the list of heroes in Donegal goes back to Red Hugh O'Donnell. More significant, however, in recent times have been the Land League, the Land Annuities campaign and the cooperative movements, led by people as diverse as Canon MacFadden of Gweedore and Peadar O'Donnell. The latter was an uncompromising socialist, who presided over the present century with a combination of literary genius and political action rarely found outside Ireland, as vocal in his criticisms of shopkeepers as of landlords, and of Franco's Fascists as of American involvement in Indo-China.

Derry too had its part to play: the most prominent heroes in the Planter tradition are the apprentices who acted on impulse to defend their citadel. Always at a distance from the seats of power, Derry, despite its London charters, was often more fiercely opposed to the bourgeois establishments of Belfast, Dublin and London than it was to the native population at its back.

It is in Derry, therefore, that we start our westward journey and with that city's James Simmons, folk-singer and poet who was born a 'well-to-do Protestant' here in 1933. Simmons was the first of a new generation of writers coming after Hewitt and Rodgers but before Heaney, Longley and Mahon. As someone who predates the Sixties, Simmons is hard to place. As someone who is at times over-influenced by the vitality of ballad forms he is occasionally hard to take seriously. But what is unmistakable is the rebellion, the need to challenge taboo, to explore the personal and the everyday to the discomfiture of those who would set limits on the territories of poetry.

In 1968 he founded the *Honest Ulsterman*, a magazine with a seminal role to play in Ulster's literary 'renaissance', the editor-ship of which was later taken over by his fellow Derry poet, Michael Foley. When the subtitle of the first *H.U.*, a *Monthly Handbook for Revolution* was brought to the attention of the authorities, Simmons's humour and his seriousness were both at play. And his focus on Judy Garland seems years ahead of others' easy identifications with Marilyn Monroe as cultural icon. The last two lines of 'In Memoriam: Judy Garland' are among the most immediate and poetic of his work:

> Discs are turning. Needles touch the rings
> Of dark rainbows. Judy Garland sings.

It is probably in *Judy Garland and the Cold War* (1976), that Simmons's writing comes of age, having become both literary and personal, addressing figures as diverse as Donne, Conrad, Tom Moore, Synge, Yeats and Bertrand Russell but in every case relating their lives to personal experience. The manifesto must surely be 'No Land is Waste', Eliot's London revisited by the artist as a young man attempting to reclaim some good in the *ordinary* – finally touching T.S. for a fiver. The same genius is at work in 'Didn't He Ramble', taking its title from the New Orleans, post-funereal stomp, the defiant, macho antiphon to Handel's 'Dead March'. Here Simmons enthuses over jazz and blues in the manner of many of his contemporaries but offers a sideswipe – 'The campus poets used to write of saxophones / disgustedly' – at the Brideshead generation who regarded Eliot's work as a clarion call to elitism.

Anyone listening to the song 'Complacency Country', Simmons's affectionate and biting comment on 'the country of boiled eggs / and butter and ham' (on *The Rostrevor Sessions* LP), must be struck by the way in which Derry saxophonist Gay MacIntyre's jazz obbligato – half township riff, half pibroch – counterpoints the poet's *beguine* rhythm. Simmons's involvement with jazz is clearly more than the predictable passing reference to popular culture for effect.

Simmons, schooled in Derry, Belfast and Leeds, is an urban poet but his 'deep rivers, dry houses / potatoes and corn' are just the setting for our trip through Prehen to Ballymagorry past small filling-stations with potatoes for sale under the dubious slogan 'British Queens the Best!' This is Planter country and it is here on the Derry/Tyrone border that 'The Field' in Sam Burnside's short story of that name is situated. The story is of a boy whose father has moved up into Derry after selling a farm that has supported his family for generations but keeping a small field on the basis that: 'You can never go wrong with a bit of land'. Burnside, born and raised in Co Antrim but living and working in Derry since the early 1970s, has a sharp insight into the feelings that underlie many of the louder political posturings so often identified with Ulster, an insight into nonconformist but strictly conforming values, long dormant memories of radicalism, the relentless undercurrents of Calvinism and the rejection of the *rootlessness* that is so much a theme for Samuel Ferguson and John Hewitt. And Burnside tackles those conflicts in the same quiet yet profound way that Hewitt pioneered, starting with self-knowledge, examining and adopting or adapting the older myths and legends and the lore of place and place-names, while cherishing what is good, decent and courageous in Ulster's people.

Burnside's heroes include James Hope, Wolfe Tone, Ferguson, Mary Ann McCracken, all those who represent radical Ulster and the spirit of Enlightenment which rose in the 1790s. But he acknowledges, too, the power of 'the cathedral' in his pamphlet of that name, and the title of his first full collection, *Walking the Marches* (1990) has an unabashed ring to it. Perhaps more than anyone he has identified the reaction of ordinary Protestant people to the Troubles. While Hewitt upbraided the 'coasters' who allowed the poisonous clouds to grow and Simmons comments, 'My uncles look back / and they call that time peace', Burnside tells, in his short story 'Voices', of an uncle who, as society around him changes, in the time post-1969, begins to hear voices, perhaps the sound of the radio, perhaps an accumulation or extension of the deadly news and the endless analysis of the Ulster situation. This is Waugh's Pinfold on the verge of chaos; the voices have just enough truth to shock the reader.

> He had discovered, he said, two sets of voices. One set spoke *of* him. From these he learned that he was narrow-minded, puritanical, prejudiced, a usurper of place, the inheritor of stolen acres, a dark-faced and black-hearted bigot who had gloried in the oppression of his neighbours and profited from it…
>
> Then he explained about the second set of voices. These spoke *for* him.

The culture-shock which a once clearly defined and justified people has undergone in less than a generation is seen as literally a state of shock, and as a result the uncle's voice, and one feels the narrator's voice, are hedged-in, characterised in an unacceptable way and therefore unwilling to speak. The result is that the generous and fair are sidelined and only the loud in that community – in any community in such circumstances – are heard. This is a theme to which Burnside returns, the evangelist's message mixing with consumerism and pop ephemera in the poem 'Coleraine Square' which records the sights and sounds of life in the North. For some the challenge has been to enfranchise a Northern Catholic voice, for others, to find a Protestant imagination. Burnside, for all his breadth of vision, his love of myth of place and his refusal to define life as a game of two sides, gives voice to a cast of mind that is too often dismissed in all the terms the old uncle hears in the passage above and too often excluded from the realms of literature.

Strabane's contribution to the written word is generally thought (though wrongly so) to be limited to the works of Cecil Frances Alexander's 'Once in Royal David's City' and 'All Things Bright and Beautiful', the latter a sentimental hymn to a conservative God. However it can claim other literary connections, among them, John Gamble, born in the town in 1770, and who produced a number of books depicting ordinary life as it was lived in the northern part of the island in the early 1800s. And Strabane was an important centre for the printing trade. John McCreery, born in 1768, was a printer who wrote poetry. Indeed, the border town has a secure place in radical history since it was here that John Dunlap, who printed the American Declaration of Independence in his newspaper, the *Pennsylvania Packet*, learned his trade in William Gray's printing shop on Main Street. In fact, a presiding spirit of the Declaration was Francis Allison, born over the border in Donegal, a pupil of Francis Hutcheson who was one of the founding figures in the Scottish Enlightenment. Allison set up a school at New London, Pennsylvania, where he was to teach Thomas McKean from Ballymoney, one of the signatories, Charles Thomson from Maghera, the first Secretary of Congress, and Ephraim Blaine, also from Donegal, who kept the supply lines open to the revolutionary troops holed-up in Valley Forge in the bitter winter of 1777. Hutcheson's liberal principles contributed, through Allison and his disciples, to that separation of Church and State which long marked the difference between American politics and its European prototypes.

As we cross the border and travel through Lifford to Raphoe we pass Ballindrait, birthplace of James Porter, later to achieve fame as the dissenting minister and United Irishman of Greyabbey, the only clergyman to hang for his alleged part in the '98 rebellion. Porter's offence had been primarily literary: his pseudonymous ballads in The *Northern Star* had lampooned the Earl of Londonderry and after the suppression of the rising he was tried by court-martial – with Londonderry among the officers – on a trumped-up charge and hanged within sight of his family's cottage.

Raphoe has a different significance in the novels of Peadar O'Donnell, however. It was here in this rich stretch of land that so many of the poor people of the Rosses and the Donegal islands found work, usually through the hiring fair at Strabane, and it is here, in *Islanders* (1928) that Nellie Doogan dies:

> They carried Nellie Doogan's coffin down the slip, and put it into the boat that had taken her to Dungloe, when she went to the hiring fair. Sally sat beside the coffin, and the women leaned forward eagerly to listen to her story of how Nellie had died from neglected appendicitis, and how she had lain all by herself, for days, in a barn loft.

Charlie, Nellie's brother eventually finds work in Raphoe and has his limited revenge on Nellie's coarse and callous employer. O'Donnell's writing however does not fall easily into cliché and in *The Knife* (1930) the story of an upwardly-mobile family from the 'servant' class in the same fertile farmland, his heroes are the liberal Protestant Doctor Henry, (who ends up in a Free-State prison as a result of his friendship with The Knife) and Sam Rowan, an Orangeman whose love for Nuala, The Knife's sister, leads him to organise a rescue party to spring the 'republicans' from their firing-squad.

Back on the road to Stranorlar and Ballybofey, then through Donegal town, and we come quickly upon Mountcharles, birthplace of Seumas MacManus, a popular writer of stories, verse and plays, now largely overlooked since his work portrayed a sentimentalised, stage-Irishry. Indeed, dividing his time between Ireland and America after his first visit there in 1899, MacManus was one of many who decried the Abbey's presentation there of Synge's *Playboy*. His first book was published in 1893, and from then until his death in 1960 his output was prolific and the titles of some of the works, *'Twas in Dhroll Donegal*, *The Humours of Donegal*, *The Resurrection of Dinny O'Dowd*, give the flavour. In 1901 he married Anna Johnston who, as the poet Ethna Carbery, had edited the nationalist magazine *The Shan Van Vocht* (1896-1899) with Alice Milligan. Her patriotic verse generated much interest after her early death in 1902, and one of her ballads, 'Roddy MacCorley', about a Presbyterian hero of the battle of Antrim, has since passed into the folk tradition.

Down to Killybegs (the centre now for a very vigorous women's writing group) and which, Joyce's Citizen tells us, was once the 'third largest harbour in the wide world': it is here among other places that the writer William Allingham worked as a Customs Officer. Born in Ballyshannon and generally more noted for his diaries and letters he was to become a friend of Tennyson, Browning, Carlyle and Rossetti, editor of *Fraser's Magazine* and a contributor to *The Athenaeum* and Dickens' *Household Words*. He was, surprisingly for a man of his background, resolutely anti-imperialist and his long poem, *Lawrence Bloomfield in Ireland* (1864) deals evenhandedly with the Land Question and the issue of evictions. Never a nationalist, he nonetheless has a rare feeling for the Donegal people in their struggles, a sympathy which shows itself in his knowledge of local traditions in *The Ballad Book* (1864) and *Evil May-Day* (1882), the latter included his best-known poem, 'The Fairies'.

The mountainy journey from Killybegs to the Glenties takes us to MacGill country, to 'Meenahalla and Strasallagh and Cagharacreen', placenames that the peasant poet relishes for their music much as Mark Twain relishes the aboriginal Australian placenames in the nonsense verses in *More Innocents Abroad*. Indeed, Patrick MacGill's *Songs of Donegal* (1921) are in similar vein to those of Seumas MacManus, but with a surer grip on the experience of the mountain poor. Leaving Mullanmore National School at the age of twelve he 'hired' at local fairs and, at fourteen, emigrated to Scotland to work with migrant potato pickers and then with itinerant labourers. At twenty he published *Gleanings from a Navvy's Scrapbook* (1911) of which he sold eight thousand copies many of them door-to-door. He moved to London in 1912 to work on the *Daily Express*, joined the London Irish Rifles later and wrote *The Great Push* (1916) in which he combines enthusiasm for his comrades, and their courage and humanity, with a questioning (which was years ahead of its time) of the morality of war.

But it is not a poet or journalist but as novelist that MacGill is best remembered: when his first novel, *Children of the Dead End* (1914), sold ten thousand copies within fifteen days, he had clearly become the voice of the oppressed in England and Scotland. His novels are more significant in terms of their outreach than, say, Walter Greenwood's *Love on the Dole*

(1933) and, although many writers and thinkers attest to the effect Tressell's novel had on their political formation, Tressell, like Orwell, and unlike MacGill, was the educated man 'slumming it'. *The Ragged-Trousered Philanthropists* provides a loose narrative structure on which the author hangs a series of sermons, disquisitions and reflections. In MacGill's novels by contrast the narrative is the message and Moleskin Joe hero of *Children of the Dead End* and eponymous hero of a later book avoids any attempt at political analysis, comment or even awareness. It is easy to see why MacGill's works were instantly popular and if the *Left Book Club* in the thirties was to create the intellectual framework for postwar socialism, MacGill's novels did much to create the *mass* support for reform.

Leaving the Glenties we cross the Gweebarra River and travel through Dungloe to Meenmore where Peadar O'Donnell was raised. Between Killybegs in the south and Bloody Foreland to the north, the north west climate and terrain is at its most unforgiving. Yet just as the people of Wales, Cornwall and the Barrow peninsula, regarded as strangers or *gall* by the rest of Anglo-Saxondom, referred to themselves as comrades, (Cumbria, Cymru), so the people of West Donegal found the solution to their problems not in arid political theory but in partnership and cooperation. The ideas of communism or shared ownership are nothing new in Ireland: Marx commented on the wisdom of communal living in the monasteries, and the indigenous form of Christianity in Ireland was indeed monastic. What is more telling is the absence of verbs of possession or ownership in Gaelic. And commentators such as de Tocqueville remarked on the fact that in hard times in Ireland it was not the landlord who supported the starving tenant but the poor who gave to the poor. It is not surprising therefore, that this area should have produced two great cooperative movements under Paddy The Cope (Gallagher), who published his autobiography, *My Story,* in 1939 and under Father James McDyer of the Glenties.

It is equally unsurprising that two of the great socialist thinkers in English letters should come from the Glenties and the Rosses and that both should seek to convey their beliefs, not by means of political tracts but by illustrating the value of comradeship in the face of hardship, in MacGill's case among the downtrodden peripatetic labourers in Scotland and England, and in O'Donnell's among the impoverished farming and fishing people of his homeplace.

It was inevitable then, that if O'Donnell supported independence pre-1916, he would be equally opposed to the rising middle-classes and their jockeying for position in the new order, whether through jobs in the civil service or through commercial and political knavery worthy of the landlords they had replaced. His loyalty to principle led him into conflict almost immediately with the Free State and with the Catholic hierarchy, since he saw the Church as adopting a position of power, abandoning the role it had enjoyed for many centuries, being both in and of the people. (This, despite the fact that Canon MacFadden gets passing mention in several novels.) The stories of O'Donnell's own escapades as a TGWU official, as civil war soldier in the Four Courts, as a resident of Mountjoy jail and as organiser of a famous strike at a mental hospital in Monaghan are numerous and often hilarious.

But his permanent legacy is in the stories of the people he knew, first as a boy in Meenmore and later as a teacher on Aranmore island. Of these, *Storm* (1925) and *The Knife* (1930) are the most concerned with the Troubles, the latter containing his political views on the 'gombeen' man and his personal belief that loyalties between friends and neighbours, regardless of creed or affiliation, are stronger than politics and politicking.

From a literary viewpoint, O'Donnell's writing breaks new ground in the use of short filmic scenes, cutting from character to character, from plot to subplot, to create pace and authenticity at a time when English and American writers were consciously over-writing and Woolf and Joyce were delving further and further into explorations of the nature of consciousness. In *Islanders* (1928) the technique is at its most assured, relying on minimal scene-setting and a firm grip of authentic dialogue which eschews sentimentality while conveying powerful emotions. At its best its simplicity prefigures the realism of Raymond Carver or Richard Ford who discovered much later the (aesthetic) power of ordinary lives as they are lived in (sometimes extraordinary) settings.

The journey back to Derry takes us past the sheer slopes of Errigal, past the Glenveagh National Park with its beauty and its tragic history; it is an impressive but lonely journey. This is country that has only ever supported a few souls, and in those places where more than a few could survive, they were ousted to make way for deer and the Romantic view. After the closeness and congestion of parts of coastal Donegal it is easy to see how that spirit of sharing grew up on the spectacular and barren coast and how its literary geniuses could write only about, and for, the people. Through Kilmacrenan to Letterkenny and we are back in the unloved Ireland of shopkeepers and publicans whom Yeats affected to despise (from the vantage point he so consciously created for himself) and whom O'Donnell and MacGill learned to distrust from their experiences gained within the class positions in which they found themselves.

Our road takes us past Burt, birthplace of W.D. Flackes, a writer of fiction but better known as a journalist and later as the BBC's Northern Ireland political correspondent. And then, a final stop at Grianan Ailigh, the former hill top residence of the O'Neill Kings of Ulster, with its stupendous views of Inishowen, the Foyle and the Swilly, Derry, the Sperrins and the Donegal mountains. The fort here is a nineteenth-century reconstruction but the imaginative visitor can see it as it was in the ninth century when timbers were drawn from Cratloe Wood near Limerick to build the superstructure, long before oaks from the same wood were taken to build London's Westminster Hall in 1399 and to roof Amsterdam's Town Hall in 1648, a year before the first siege of Derry and 40 years before William left Holland for Brixham. But even before that Grianan existed as a site for cultures now lost to history. The place holds a fascination for anyone interested in the highly sophisticated Gaelic culture which all but disappeared in the last few centuries, leaving the incoming Planter with the feeling, no doubt, that he would have to carve his existence out of barren rock. Hewitt, who, more than most, has explored and defined the mindset of the Planter, acknowledges that earlier world in 'Clogh-Oir', 'one of three / Sacred Stones when queens sunned at Ailech'. It is from here then that we allow Sam Burnside to take us on the last stretch of the round trip with these lines from his poem 'Grianan of Aileach to Derry - 21 December':

> At its farthest limit the winter sun
> Stiffens into a stillness…
> All breathing ceases in this stark confrontation
> Of all the earth's bright days and all dark nights.

V

Crossing the Seven Streams

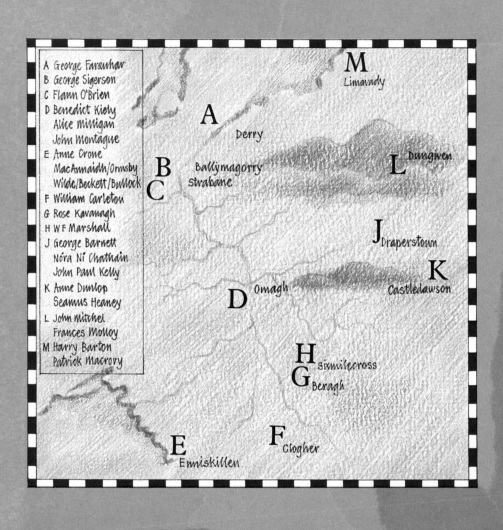

A George Farquhar
B George Sigerson
C Flann O'Brien
D Benedict Kiely
  Alice Milligan
  John Montague
E Anne Crone
  MacAnnaidh/Ormsby
  Wilde/Beckett/Bullock
F William Carleton
G Rose Kavanagh
H W F Marshall
J George Barnett
  Nóra Ní Chathain
  John Paul Kelly
K Anne Dunlop
  Seamus Heaney
L John Mitchel
  Frances Molloy
M Harry Barton
  Patrick Macrory

M Limavady

A Derry

L Dungiven

B Ballymagorry
C Strabane

J Draperstown

K Castledawson

D Omagh

H Sixmilecross
G Beragh

F Clogher

E Enniskillen

Crossing the Seven Streams:
Writers from Foyle to Erne

Marion Ross

During a journey that takes her from one famous body of water (the Foyle) to another (the Erne) and over roads that make their way through three counties, Marion Ross travels southwards from one ancient place (Derry) to another (Enniskillen) and then north and eastwards back across the lonely Sperrin Mountains. Along the way she crosses many rivers and bridges; during her journey she discovers and revels in the rich and diverse work of many writers who speak out of and for many cultures. Some of these men and women are of world stature, some of local repute, some, indeed, almost forgotten; yet, in her subsequent reading of their work Marion Ross uncovers a gift they shared for responding to place, to people and to the energy of language, and for doing so with humour and wit. In discussing what in any terms is a remarkable body of talent she examines, among others, the warm folk humour of W.F. Marshall, the sparkling wit of Wilde, the black humour of Beckett (and of Flann O'Brien), the indefatigable inclination to laughter shown by Carleton, Kiely and MacAnniadh, the zany narratives of Anne Dunlop and the tragi-comic world of Frances Molloy. Appropriately, she begins by discussing the work of Derry-born George Farquhar, one of the best known writers of late-Restoration comedy.

A literary journey beginning in the city of Londonderry and wending its way through the varied, and often dramatic, landscapes of Counties Londonderry, Tyrone and Fermanagh, involves the shedding of many popular preconceptions. In the first instance, the area is often viewed as a cultural backwater where the harsh realities of life in an impoverished, if scenically beautiful area, are deemed to intrude upon and even stifle the creative imagination.

Secondly, the enduring nature of the region's political problems seem as depressingly present today, (again, a time of great upheaval in the political order of Europe), as they did when Winston Churchill remarked upon them in his 1929 treatise on political Europe in the aftermath of the Great War of 1914-18:

> The whole map of Europe has been changed. The mode and thought of men, the whole outlook on affairs, the grouping of parties, all have encountered violent and tremendous changes in the deluge of the world, but as the deluge subsides and the waters fall, we see the dreary steeples of Fermanagh and Tyrone emerging once again. The integrity of their quarrel is one of the few institutions that has been left unaltered in the cataclysm which has swept the world.

Daunting words; words suggestive of a community torn apart by ancient enmities, with little time or energy left to nurture a thriving and vital literary tradition. Happily, the opposite is the case for, as I discovered during my journey through these three counties, there is a wealth of fine and serious literature emanating from this particular corner of the province of Ulster. It is a body of literature given to us by both native and visiting writers; inspired in some instances by reaction and resistance to old political wrongs and grievances; in others, by a deep, almost spiritual sense and love of place. But, in the main, imbued, as I soon found to my delight, with that most Irish of characteristics, defined by Vivian Mercier in *The Irish Comic Tradition* (1962), as 'a bent for wild humour, a delight in witty word play and a tendency to regard satire as one of the indispensable functions of the literary man'.

It is appropriate then that we begin inside the city walls with George Farquhar, pupil at the Free Grammar School of Londonderry, around the time of what the historian Macaulay, termed 'the most memorable siege in the annals of the British Isles'. Farquhar was born in Derry in 1677 when his mother, the wife of a Reverend Farquhar, a clergyman officially titled the 'Prebendary of Raphoe', travelled to the town in order to obtain 'superior medical assistance' for the birth of her child. Little is known about Farquhar's early childhood but it is probable that at the age of seven or eight he was enrolled as a pupil at the Free Grammar School, the forerunner of today's Foyle and Londonderry College, at that time sited within the city walls, in Schoolhouse Lane, near present day Society Street.

Farquhar's education was probably interrupted by the siege of Derry which started during the winter of 1688 and ended in the summer of 1689. Almost certainly, the school closed and presumably young George took refuge in his family home but even there he was witness to the horrors attendant upon the siege. Following the preservation of Derry, the defeated troops of James II plundered and burnt the rectory of Farquhar's father. Shortly afterwards, the unfortunate man 'burnt out of all that he had', died of grief. It was in response to this, it is believed, that George Farquhar, then 13 years old, volunteered with other boys of his age to join the Williamite camp, and he is reputed to have been at the Battle of the Boyne in 1690.

In 1691, the Free Grammar School re-opened and the education of Farquhar resumed. His literary talents flourished and in 1694 he gained entrance to Trinity College, Dublin. However, his time at Trinity was undistinguished and he left in 1696 to take up an acting career in Dublin's Smock Alley Theatre. An accident during a performance of Dryden's *The Indian Emperor*, whereby he forgot to use a blunted sword and wounded a fellow actor, though 'not dangerously', brought this period of Farquhar's life to an abrupt halt.

Intending to make his fortune as a playwright he proceeded to London with the script of a comedy, *Love and a Bottle*. This was staged in 1698 and achieved a moderate success. However, his next play, *The Constant Couple*, premièred in November 1699, was a major triumph. Three failures followed in quick succession, bringing Farquhar to the brink of financial ruin. His last two comedies, however, are his finest. The material for *The Recruiting Officer* was obtained as a result of his experiences as a recruiter for an army regiment. First performed in April, 1706, it provided its author with a small measure of financial security. However, this was short-lived and *The Beaux Stratagem*, Farquhar's final comedy, was written in circumstances of the greatest need. Farquhar's health was also failing during the writing of the play, and he died shortly after the acclaimed first performance of his masterpiece, at the tragically young age of twenty-nine.

As witnessed by their long stage history (*The Beaux Stratagem* playing recently to enthusiastic audiences in the West End of London), the best of Farquhar's comedies have withstood the vicissitudes of taste rather well. Sparkling wit, original dialogue, memorable characters such as Lady Bountiful, Captain Plume, Sergeant Kite and Boniface, whose name has entered theatrical history as a generic term for an innkeeper, have secured their status as masterpieces of the Restoration comic tradition. Whilst retaining many standard Restoration devices in his comedies, the bawdiness so typical of the genre is certainly present in his dialogue, as is the inclination to portray love affairs as revolving solely around the finances of marriage and the choice of a socially suitable partner – Farquhar also broke new ground. Rejecting the tendency for plays of the tradition to be overwhelmingly urban and metropolitan in setting and outlook, he offered his audiences something decidedly different – an entertaining and, unusual for the time, sympathetic portrayal of small town and country life.

Farquhar's themes are diverse and topical. In *The Beaux Stratagem*, for instance, he discusses the nature of gentility on the one hand, and on the other, allows his characters to debate marriage and divorce in passages whose source can only be Milton's great, and intensely controversial, pamphlet *The Doctrine and Discipline of Divorce* (1643). The subject matter is weighty but the tone is witty, resourceful and intelligent, and it is no small measure of Farquhar's lasting greatness as a playwright that his ability to speak eloquently and satisfyingly to his audience is still a potent factor almost three centuries later.

Leaving the city behind, our journey onwards to Strabane offers some of the most delightful scenery of our trip. Across the River Foyle, the beautiful plain of Raphoe stretches out before us, an idyllic landscape of bright green water-meadows, interspersed with trees and elegant Georgian dwelling houses. Small rounded hills shelter humbler abodes whilst, in the distance, the blue-grey shadowed profiles of the hills of Donegal preside over the magical scene below.

On the Northern Ireland side of the river, just before we come to the small village of Ballymagorry, we take a left turn and arrive at Holyhill, the birthplace of George Sigerson, scholar, poet and scientist. Born on 11 January 1836, the second youngest of six children, he was the son of a prosperous landowner. Sigerson's early education was received at the local Glebe School and the Academy in Letterkenny, Co. Donegal. In 1852 his father sent him to Paris to join his brother and he returned to Ireland in 1855, laden down with prizes and awards. He proceeded to Queen's College, Galway and then to Cork to study for his medical degree. An illustrious academic career followed and his research so impressed Charles Darwin that he nominated him for membership of the Linnean Society. Sigerson also translated Charcot's *Diseases of the Nervous System*, adding valuable notes of his own.

But Sigerson's interests were not confined to the realm of science. His childhood, in the beautiful valley of the Glenmornan River, had awakened in him a deep and abiding love for the Irish language. Tyrone, in the early part of the nineteenth century, still had a sizable Gaelic speaking community, and many of the farm labourers or 'mountainy men' who visited the Sigerson spade foundry were fluent native speakers. Young George became intrigued and fascinated by the musicality of their conversations and was soon stimulated to learn the language.

Thus began what was to become a life-long interest in Irish literature. Sigerson must have been conscious, at many points, of a divided allegiance within him between scientific and literary matters. For, at much the same time as he was furthering the cause of medical research, he was building up a significant literary reputation. By 1860, Sigerson was already established as a Gaelic translator and, in that year, the publication of his first book, *The Poets and Poetry of Munster*, was heralded as an event of national importance. By the mid-sixties, Sigerson was contributing many articles, poems – both originals and translations – stories, essays and political writings to the leading journals and periodicals of the day.

Sigerson published his most important work in the field of translation in 1897, an anthology of Irish verse entitled *Bards of the Gael and Gall*. This traced Irish verse from its beginnings right up to the contemporary period, and involved an ambitious effort, on the part of Sigerson, to find a mode of writing in English which would do justice to the complexity of the Gaelic original. As noted in the *Field Day Anthology of Irish Writing*, this 'forced Sigerson, as it later forced others, to abandon some of the conventions of contemporary poetry and to replace them with more direct and colloquial speech and rhythms'. Synge, Colum, F.R. Higgins and others were obvious and immediate beneficiaries of Sigerson's success in this task.

But the nature of Sigerson's contribution to Irish literature is best voiced by Douglas Hyde who, in his diaries, identifies George Sigerson as the dominant figure among literary nationalists because, unlike O'Leary and Yeats, whose objective was to promote the anti-imperialist struggle through their writings, Sigerson was more interested in saving the language and the stories which were disappearing with it. In Hyde's view, no living Irishman had done more to preserve the oral tradition than Sigerson.

We journey into Strabane the town where the well-known Ulster expression 'Tyrone among the bushes', has its origins, and is to be found in a poem written by William Collins, a local poet and novelist who was born in 1838. The poem begins:

> O God be with the good old time when I was twenty-one,
> In Tyrone amongst the bushes, where the Finn and Mourne run,
> When my heart was gay and merry, recked then not of care and toil,
> Blithesome as the bells of Derry ringing o'er the sunny Foyle.

In more recent times, however, Strabane is noted as the birthplace of Brian O'Nolan who wrote under a plethora of pseudonyms: Myles na gCopaleen, Brother Barnabas, Count O'Blather to name but a few, but achieved fame principally as Flann O'Brien, the author of the comic masterpiece *At Swim-Two-Birds* (1939).

Surprisingly, given O'Nolan's track record as a master of mysteries and evasions, his early childhood is fairly well documented. He was born on 5 October 1911 at 15 Bowling Green, Strabane. His father, an Irish speaker, was an officer in the Customs and Excise Service, and in the course of his work was often moved around the country. Eventually, the family settled in Blackrock, a seaside suburb of Dublin, and it was here that O'Nolan wrote his earliest (and perhaps his finest) work.

Central to O'Nolan's work is a vision not unlike that of Beckett or Kafka. If man, he argues, 'has the courage to raise his eyes and look sanely at the awful human condition…he must realise finally that tiny periods of temporary release from intolerable suffering is the most that any individual has the right to expect'. And release, for O'Nolan, as is also the case with Beckett and Kafka, is to be obtained through laughter. If life is just 'comic maggot folly', then the proper way to treat it is as a comedy. Moreover, satire could actually improve the world by pricking the bubbles of pomposity, hypocrisy and philistinism which were everywhere in evidence. Laughter, then, is both a consolation and a defence against the horror of living.

And the forms which allow O'Nolan to induce this therapeutic laughter involve, as the critic Anne Clissman has pointed out, the creation of fantasy worlds, of situations which bear a disturbing, sideways relation to reality but in which everything is possible. The imagination is allowed to roam at will. Emphasis is placed on the erratic, the new combination of facts, the surprising perspective and the work points, by way of a vision which often appears darkly insane, to sanity and balance – a 'sane madness' as O'Nolan himself termed it. The realistic, mundane and moralistic tradition of novel writing is eschewed and O'Nolan sets out, like the ancient Gaelic poets, to remove himself from the distractions of the present and to spin, in the unassailable privacy of his own mind, a 'storyteller's book web'.

And in *At Swim-Two-Birds* he achieves this in superb and hilarious fashion. To the uninitiated it is, at first, a puzzling book. The title, for instance, turns out to be the translation of an Irish place name *Snámh-dá-én*, a small place on the river Shannon, which was visited by mad Sweeney, a character who appears in a 12th-century Irish tale, and also in the novel. The first page of the book involves three separate openings, and before long we are in the midst of three separate worlds, all of them bizarre. But above all, *At Swim-Two-Birds* is a supremely funny book, replete with amusing characters and situations, and hilarious exposés of various literary conventions. But any attempt to pigeon-hole a book where one of the characters the narrator is writing about is also writing a book about a motley group of characters who lead their independent lives when he is asleep is doomed to instant failure. The only directive must be, read and re-read the book and experience the delights at first-hand.

Following the publication of *At Swim-Two-Birds* O'Nolan's output was varied and plentiful. *The Third Policeman* (1967); *The Hard Life* (1961); *The Dalkey Archive* (1964); *An Béal Bocht* (1941) – the English version, *The Poor Mouth,* was published in 1973 – and numerous television scripts, plays and short stories were published and met with mixed reactions. Co-existing with the Flann O'Brien persona, however, was Myles na gCopaleen, the author of a humorous column in *The Irish Times* – the incomparable 'Cruiskeen Lawn' [the full little jug]; in this he entertained an avid following with side-splitting tales on any and every subject during the years 1939 to 1966. Finally, the year 1939 also saw the publication of the novel *Oíche i nGleann na nGealt*, written by another member of the O'Nolan family, Brian's brother Ciarán.

Leaving Strabane, we pass through the 'model' village of Sion Mills and enter open country. The road runs alongside the Mourne River, whose broad waters tumble and rush through the rocks for a time, and then, tranquillity restored, flows softly onwards. Just before we reach Newtownstewart, the road branches off to Baronscourt, the fine Georgian home of the Duke and Duchess of Abercorn. The Duchess of Abercorn is a direct descendent of Alexander Pushkin, Russia's most celebrated poet. To mark this connection schoolchildren compete annually for the prestigious Pushkin Prizes which have been established to encourage creative writing.

Past Newtownstewart, the Mourne River merges with the Strule, and we travel onwards to Omagh, glimpsing, at times, the brooding stillness and loneliness of the Gortin Glen Forest as it straddles the horizon. Omagh is situated where the rivers Camowen and Drumragh unite to form the Strule. Architecturally interesting, the almost continental tableau created by the twin-towered Catholic church and the tall, narrow houses huddled about its foot, contrasts strangely with the Georgian character of the main street, topped by the classical style courthouse. Omagh is built on hills, and Benedict Kiely, in his account of his Omagh boyhood and young manhood, *Drink to the Bird* (1991) recreates the view from Cannonhill.

> If you looked back from Cannonhill, the prospect, or perhaps it should be the retrospect, was really something; the whole Town, spires and all, you could even see clear down into some of the streets; the winding river or rivers, the red brick of the county hospital…as also Arethusa Glenhordial of the pure mountain springs, and Gortin Gap and Mullagharn and the tips of Sawel and Dart in the high Sperrins.

Benedict Kiely, short story writer, novelist, critic, journalist and broadcaster was born on 15 August 1919, near Dromore in Co Tyrone. Kiely received his education in the Christian Brothers School in the town. At that time, Omagh was a garrison town, and he recalls that 'Bugles from the military barracks divided the day as do bells in a monastery. The barracks stood like a medieval fortress on a high-walled place above the loops of the Strule'. Indeed, the dominating presence of the British army barracks and the Catholic church steeples were to provide Kiely with opposing symbols for his novels and stories. Yet, although Kiely belonged to the Catholic and Nationalist tradition, relationships with his Protestant neighbours and even the soldiers were amicable. In a recent interview he explains that, 'There was very little religious antagonism. Nor isn't to this day. We were all friends and neighbours in our street'.

Clearly, Benedict Kiely has happy associations with Omagh and with 'the green flowery banks of the serpentine Strule' which flows through it. The Omagh region figures prominently in his work and provides the setting for his first two novels, *Land Without Stars* (1946) and *In a Harbour Green* (1949). Evidently, his writing debut was prompted by his discovery of and admiration for an earlier Co Tyrone writer, William Carleton; and Kiely's critical biography of Carleton, entitled *Poor Scholar* (1947) led directly to a revival of interest in the work of his literary predecessor. Moreover, Carleton has greatly influenced Kiely's prose. The speaking voice of the storyteller is paramount in the work of both writers, rooting them firmly in the great Irish oral tradition. Another similarity stems from the sheer exuberance and vitality of their writing, a veritable brimming over of narrative and anecdotal energies which threatens, at times, to overwhelm the constraints of form.

As the critic John Wilson Foster has noted, Benedict Kiely, like James Joyce and Flann O'Brien, 'is heir to the archaic Irish comic tradition characterised by linguistic verve, inventiveness of plot (to the extent of fantasy on occasions), and satiric impulse'. The early novels exhibit some of these characteristics, but it is not until the publication of *Dogs Enjoy the Morning* (1968) that a tendency towards philosophical seriousness is replaced by a 'full-blooded but debunking caricature of the absurdities and extremities of human nature'. But the short stories provide, perhaps, the best vehicle for one of the dominant elements of Kiely's writing – his humour. Several collections have been published including *A Journey to the Seven Streams* (1963), *A Ball of Malt and Madame Butterfly* (1973) and *A Cow in the House* (1978). All are packed with memorable Irish figures, comic anecdotes and blunt ironies.

More recent years have seen a fictional departure for Kiely with the publication of *Proxopera* (1977) and *Nothing Happens in Carmincross* (1985), both vehement denunciations of terrorism in Northern Ireland. The novella, *Proxopera*, tells the story of a family returning from holiday in Donegal to find their home taken over by a gang of 'mad' patriots. It emerges that their cowardly plan involves forcing the grandfather, who has a delicate heart condition, to drive the family car into town, there to place a proxy bomb. Through the long night of waiting for the morning departure time and throughout the drive to town, Granda Binchey reflects on the joys as well as the sorrows of the past sixty years. The joys embracing his marriage, his family, and the white house he had coveted as a child and now owns. The sorrows: the people and surroundings destroyed by terrorist activities, the lake polluted by a political corpse and the peace of a graveyard shattered by a booby-trapped wreath. It is a forceful, serious story as is the later novel, *Nothing Happens in Carmincross* and both serve to highlight Kiely's personal, humanitarian and political philosophy. As Grace Eckley notes in an article on Kiely, it is a philosophy which allows religious tolerance, speaks of a political system broad enough to include differences and proclaims a love of nature, an attachment to the soil and to the legends that spring from it and from its people.

Just as Kiely's words introduce us to the town of Omagh so also does he introduce us to Alice Milligan, 'a great lady and a poet, the two in one'. In 1940, Alice Milligan was seventy-four years of age and during that year Ben Kiely paid many visits to the old rectory in Mountfield where she lived. They spoke of Yeats and Lady Gregory, of the early days of the Abbey Theatre and of the Irish Literary Theatre (where her verse play, *The Last Feast of the Fianna* (1900) had been produced); they spoke too of Patrick Pearse and Thomas MacDonagh and of wonderful days Alice had spent in County Donegal with Maud Gonne. Although teased about his visits, Kiely regarded them as 'a paying of tribute to a great woman, neglected by her country and her countrymen'.

Alice Milligan was born in Omagh, into a Methodist family, the daughter of Seaton Milligan, a wealthy businessman and antiquarian. Incidentally, her sister, Charlotte Milligan Fox, developed an interest in another sphere of Irish culture, and went on to found the Irish Folksong Society. The family lived in a house, with a large garden, which stood in the sharp angle between the Killyclogher Road and the Asylum Road. Undoubtedly, it was this garden that was in Alice's memory when she wrote one of her best known poems:

> When I was a little girl,
> In a garden playing,
> A thing was often said
> To chide us from delaying:
>
> When after sunny hours,
> At twilight's falling,
> Down through the garden walks
> Came our old nurse calling,
>
> 'Come in! for it's growing late,
> And the grass will wet ye!
> Come in! or when it's dark
> The Fenians will get ye'.

The nurse is intent upon striking fear into the children and when they reach the shelter of home she relates a tale of 'a night in March when an army of Papists grim came devastating'. The situation was dire but intervention, of the divine sort, was to save the day.

> But God (Who our nurse declared
> Guards British dominions)
> Sent down a deep fall of snow
> And scattered the Fenians.

The nurse is not convinced, however, that they have been vanquished and, such is her disquiet, that the children, frightened still, cry to be tucked into bed. All except Alice, the 'one little rebel' who,

> Watching all with laughter,
> Thought 'When the Fenians come
> I'll rise and go after.'

And go after, she did, dedicating her life and her work to the nationalist cause. Her love of the Irish language, sparked off by her visits with her uncle to the hiring fairs in County Tyrone where transactions were carried out in Gaelic, was immense. From 1896 to 1899, she and Ethna Carbery edited the nationalist and literary magazine *The Shan Van Vocht* in Belfast. In 1898, she was involved in her first production of a play in Irish, in the town of Letterkenny.

Her literary output was prolific, if uneven in quality. The subject matter of her early verse dealt with scenery and legend, whilst the later work from *Hero Lays* (1908) onwards concentrated on historical and nationalistic themes. She was devastated by the death of her friends and fellow nationalists in the 1916 Rising, and equally saddened by the Civil War of 1922-23. The poem 'Till Ferdia Came' articulates her despair as brother is set against brother, 'two valiant sons of one fond mother'. She wrote little after the Treaty and died on 13 April, 1953. On her gravestone, in the ancient graveyard of Drumragh, just outside Omagh, is the simple inscription: *Alice L. Milligan*, and the words, written in Irish and in English, 'She loved no other place but Ireland.'

Another poet with firm roots in the area around Omagh is John Montague. He was born in Brooklyn, New York, but his childhood years were spent on his aunt's farm in County Tyrone. One of the characteristics of Montague's poetry is his sharp eye for visual detail and his deft observation comes across acutely in 'The Water Carrier', a poem in which the poet looks back on his childhood on the farm where, 'A bramble rough path ran to the river / Where one stepped carefully across slime-topped stones, / With corners abraded as bleakly white as bones.'

Later poems, however, find him viewing country life rather differently. In 'Like Dolmens Round My Childhood, The Old People' he gives five examples of Irish country life. From Maggie Owens, a lonely old gossip, to Wild Billy Harbinson, who forsook his loyalist background when all his family passed on, and 'married a Catholic servant girl', all are victims of creeds and old hatreds which destroy life and joy. The young poet must exorcise them and does so, in splendid fashion:

> Ancient Ireland, indeed! I was reared by her bedside,
> The rune and the chant, evil eye and averted head,
> Fomorian fierceness of family and local feud.
> Gaunt figures of fear and of friendliness,
> For years they trespassed on my dreams,
> Until once, in a standing circle of stones,
> I felt their shadows pass
> Into that dark permanence of ancient forms.

In a major work, *The Rough Field* (1972) Montague tackles the Northern conflict. It is an ambitious undertaking, elaborate in its sectioning, epic in its range and yet oddly personal, in so far as Montague uses the example of his family and others close to him, in addition to the more usual method of recounting historical events, to examine the particular disintegration of Ulster's culture. Written over a period of ten years, he utilises poems previously published. 'Like Dolmens Round My Childhood', for instance, recurs in the section 'Home Again', where Montague attempts to come to terms with Ulster after his many years of exile; its harsh tone counterbalanced by the touching tribute to his dying aunt in the next section, 'The Leaping Fire'. And other sections follow, tracing Ulster's past and present in rich and complex verse full of wit and irony: but, the most moving aspect of the work must remain those parts where Montague evokes memories of his divided and, in many ways betrayed, family.

Another literary figure who has connections with Omagh is Brian Friel who was born in the town. However, Friel moved to Derry when he was a young boy and is more usually associated with that city and with west Donegal (the location of the Ballybeg of many of his plays) and with Inishowen where he now lives. Robin Glendinning, the contemporary playwright and short story writer, also has links with the town, having taught for eleven years at Omagh Academy. Similarly, Patrick Boyle, may well have found that his stint as a bank manager in Omagh provided at least some of the material for his novel *Like Any Other Man* (1966) which is set in a provincial town, and also for many of his really quite excellent short stories. Finally, in the realm of folk art, Wilson Guy, a native of Fintona, adapted the persona of an old *besom-man*, Mat Mulcaghey, who had sold his crude but effective sweeping-brushes in the area, and under his assumed name, wrote rhymes, told stories and even contributed regularly to a local newspaper, the *Tyrone Constitution*.

Enniskillen beckons and the road to Dromore allows us to view the voluptuous curves of the Tyrone landscape. Through the quiet village and on past Irvinestown, the road tree-lined and the hedges thick with fuchsia. Finally, Enniskillen (Inis Ceithleann; or Ceithle's Island), the name derived from a legendary woman-warrior of around 2000 BC, who is reputed to have been, with her husband Balor, a leader of pirates from overseas, the Fomorians. Situated on the River Erne, at the junction of two great lakes, Upper Lough Erne and Lower Lough Erne, Enniskillen and the surrounding lakelands have provided inspiration for many writers.

Anne Crone has written two fine novels about Fermanagh, *Bridie Steen* (1948) and *This Pleasant Lea* (1951); these are remarkable not only for the strength of her characterisation but also for her ability to re-create vividly the farms, bogs and waters of Fermanagh. Both these features are also present in the work of Shan Bullock who was born in 1865 in Crom, South Fermanagh, where his father was a steward on the Earl of Erne's estate. After leaving school, Bullock went to London to work in the civil service, and these two vastly different worlds, London and Fermanagh, provide the material for much of his fiction. *Thomas Andrews, Shipbuilder* (1912) the story of the man who built the Titanic and lost his life when it sank, *The Loughsiders* (1924) and *By Thrasna River: The Story of a Townland* (1895) are some of his best novels, whilst the collection of short stories *The Awkward Squads* (1893) offers many insights into Ulster life at the end of the last century. Similarly, the autobiographical *After Sixty Years* (1931) is an invaluable and often moving account of Bullock's childhood in Fermanagh depicting, through his father's recollections, life in Ireland before the Famine and the Land Acts, and also by way of his own recollections, the demise of the Big House. In the same volume, Bullock also mentions that, although he was a Protestant, 'it would be always the barefooted, ragged Catholic, with his hair through his cap and only a bit of oaten bread in his pocket, that (he) was drawn to for play or company', not least because they generally 'had five or six pretty sisters in tow'.

Three other Fermanagh writers deserve mention. John Macken, who died in Enniskillen in 1823, published poetry under the name of Ismael Fitzadam. T.R.J. Polson, an editor of the *Fermanagh Mail* for many years, wrote *The Fortune Teller's Intrigue* (1847): a long novel, running to three volumes, it is set in the Ireland of the late 1700s. Finally, there is Cahir Healy, who combined a career as a civil servant with his duties as a Nationalist M.P. A native of Donegal, Healy moved to Fermanagh as a child. His literary output includes poetry (written with Cathal O'Byrne), as well as the novels, *A Sower of the Wind* (1910) and *The Escapades of Condy Corrigan*. The latter was published in America in 1910.

Recent-day Enniskillen has an abundance of talented and contemporary writers. Two poets spring to mind – Frank Ormsby and John Kelly. Born in Co Fermanagh (and educated at St Michael's College in the town), Ormsby comes from a rural Catholic background and was the first in his family to be educated beyond primary school level. In the poem 'Winter Offerings', from the largely autobiographical collection *A Store of Candles* (1977), he candidly and poignantly acknowledges the debt he owes his mother:

> Often I wonder
> How you prevailed against that blunderbuss
>
> My father. What-was-good-enough-for-him-
> The peasant's caution rather than a ploy
> To keep me tethered; but you saw how grim
> The prospects. Trapped yourself, you rescued me
> From lives I guess at. Then, how could I joy
>
> In love so functional, how call it love
> That hid and whispered in a tough concern
> With grants and benefits? So, schooled above
> You, I grew up to miss those transferred yearnings.
> School's out, but now in retrospect I learn.

Ormsby's second collection *A Northern Spring* (1986) contains a sequence of thirty-six poems about the American military presence at home, in Europe and in Northern Ireland in Spring, 1944. Written in monologue form, each American GI tells a tale: some funny, some moving, some macabre, a fascinating exploration of the ironies, the horrors and also the consolations of war.

John Kelly, broadcaster, musician, poet and prose writer – his first novel
Grace Notes and Bad Thoughts will be published in late 1994 – is also a
native of Enniskillen. An incisive wit and vivid imagination are the hallmarks
of John Kelly's poetry and both these characteristics are clearly present in
these lines from his poem 'The Day William Butler Yeats Was On the Bus':

> William Butler Yeats
> sat beside me
> on the Enniskillen bus;
>
> listening to a personal stereo,
> hands clamped to his ears,
> he caught me looking at him
> and he leaned over -
> his nose went the whole way down his face -
> Yeah! he said, Rave on! Rave on!

Two talented writers of prose come next – Carlo Gebler and Séamas
MacAnnaidh. Gebler is not a native of Fermanagh, although he now lives
and works in the county. The son of the novelist and short-story writer Edna
O'Brien, Gebler has published several critically acclaimed works. These
include the novels *August in July* (1986), *Work and Play* (1988), *Malachy
and His Family* (1990) and *Life of a Drum* (1991). His first work of non-
fiction, *Driving Through Cuba*, was published in 1988. His second venture
in this field, *The Glass Curtain* (1991) subtitled *Inside An Ulster Community*,
examines the aftermath of the Remembrance Sunday bomb at the war
memorial in Enniskillen, an atrocity which killed eleven townspeople and
severely injured a further sixty-three. Employing a lively, anecdotal style,
Gebler journeys around Enniskillen and Fermanagh, interviewing
personalities on both sides of the political and religious divide. Diary entries
and speculation are also employed to great effect and in so far as he comes
to a conclusion it is that the glass curtain of division is always there, although
it is not always obvious.

The Enniskillen born Séamas MacAnnaidh writes novels and short
stories and is considered to be in the vanguard of creative writers popularising
the Irish language for a new generation. His autobiographical trilogy
Cuaifeach Mo Londubh Buí (1983), *Mo Dhá Mhicí* (1986) and *Rubble na
Mickies* (1990) (translated the titles read, *The Whirlpool of My Yellow
Blackbird, Me Two Mickies* and *The Rubble of the Mickies*) has been widely
acclaimed. The trilogy was followed by the 1992, *Féirín, Scéalta agus Eile
(A Gift, Stories etc.)*. The blackbird is a motif which has been consciously
adopted by MacAnnaidh symbolising, for him, not only nature but also
music and poetry. He recounts a story, however, of the fate it suffered when
the first part of his trilogy was published in Russian – somehow in translation,
the yellow blackbird became a ginger thrush!

MacAnnaidh cites Strabane's Flann O'Brien, together with the Donegal writer Seosamh Mac Grianna, as strong influences and certainly echoes of the experimental style of *At Swim-Two-Birds* can be discerned in his novels and short stories. Humour is also a predominant feature as MacAnnaidh, whether journeying round his native Enniskillen or in more contemplative mood, discovers the unusual perspective which leads him into the realms of fantasy and hilarity. Unlike O'Brien, however, his central vision is firmly optimistic and the qualities which shine through in his writing are enjoyment, verve and exuberant energy.

Set on a hill on the western outskirts of Enniskillen is Portora Royal School, which was founded in 1608 by James I. A splendid building on an imposing site, Portora has produced many eminent 'old boys', including two extremely distinguished figures in the field of literature – Oscar Wilde and Samuel Beckett. Or, to amend that statement slightly by reference to Richard Ellman's comment in his definitive biography of Oscar Wilde (published in 1987): 'No school on earth produced Oscar Wilde. But Portora, which flourishes still, must be credited with having prepared not only Wilde but Samuel Beckett.'

Wilde had considerable academic success at Portora. In 1870 he was awarded the Carpenter prize for Greek Testament. In the following year he was awarded a Royal School scholarship to Trinity College, Dublin, and his name was duly inscribed in gilt letters on the school notice-board. In 1895, the year Wilde was tried and convicted for homosexual offences, his name was removed from the notice-board at Portora, and the initials O.W. which he had carved by the window of a classroom were scraped away by the headmaster. Today, his name has been restored to the honours board and regilded.

Born in Dublin on 16 October 1854, of eccentric, even notorious parents, Wilde's school-days in Portora were but the first steps in a glittering path which led, by way of Trinity College and Oxford, to the drawing rooms of London. Once there, he very quickly made a name for himself as the wittiest and most outrageous figure on the literary scene. Success as an author, however, was a little slower in coming. Short of funds, he organised a sensational lecture tour in America in 1882, but his first play, *Vera*, staged in New York the following year, was a miserable failure.

The publication of *The Happy Prince and Other Tales* in May 1888 and two essays *Pen, Pencil and Poison* and *The Decay of Lying*, in January 1889, ushered in a period of outstanding success and glory. *The Picture of Dorian Gray*, first published in *Lippincott's Monthly Magazine*, appeared as a novel in 1891. A scarcely veiled attack on conventional morality, it achieved cult status. Elsewhere, in his essays, 'The Critic as Artist' and 'The Decay of Lying', Wilde had been instrumental in revising and perfecting aestheticism; replacing the crude maxim 'Art for Art's Sake' with a much more complex and, indeed, subversive theory. The age does not shape art,

Wilde argues, but it is art which gives the age its character. Secondly, life imitates art not vice versa as has often been claimed – life is the mirror and art the reality. And Wilde's final revelation is that 'Lying, the telling of beautiful untrue things, is the proper aim of Art'. However, *Dorian Gray*, as Richard Ellman observes, is 'the aesthetic novel par excellence, not in espousing the doctrine, but in exhibiting its dangers'. What Wilde did 'was to write the tragedy of aestheticism. It was also premonitory of his own tragedy, for Dorian has like Wilde experimented with two forms of sexuality, love of women and of men. The life of mere sensation is uncovered as anarchic and self-destructive. Dorian Gray is a test case. He fails. Life cannot be lived on such terms'.

But tragedy had not quite caught up with Oscar Wilde, four golden years were to intervene. *Lady Windermere's Fan*, produced in London in 1892, was an outstanding success. It was followed by a number of plays including the classic, *The Importance of Being Earnest* (first produced 1893). And, ironically, just at the point when he was writing his best work, the society he had so often and so eloquently vilified, took its revenge. He was prosecuted and convicted on the charge of indecent behaviour with men and sentenced to two years of hard labour. The hardships of prison life, and his subsequent exile in France and Italy, left Wilde a broken man. Slighted by many of his acquaintances, unable to sustain his previous spendthrift existence, he drifted aimlessly. On his release from prison he wrote *The Ballad of Reading Gaol* (1898) and after that nothing. He died on 30 November 1900 in an obscure Paris hotel. His monument bears this inscription from *The Ballad of Reading Gaol*:

> And alien tears will fill for him
> Pity's long-broken urn,
> For his mourners will be outcast men,
> And outcasts always mourn.

Oscar Wilde once remarked that he put his genius into his life, his talent into his work. But the best of his work: *The Ballad of Reading Gaol*, a few sparkling essays, the fairy stories, *De Profundis* (a sort of testament written in prison to his lover, Lord Alfred Douglas) and the four later plays, especially *The Importance of Being Earnest*, will survive, as he had claimed that it would. However, the true measure of his greatness is the anticipation which is conjured up when his name is mentioned, the sure knowledge that what is quoted will surprise and delight us. Surprise us because, like Blake and Nietzsche, he was intent upon dismantling the flawed and severe ethics of the society in which he lived and replacing it with a morality of sympathy for society's victims. And delight us for many reasons: for the elegance of his assault upon society which, very often, initially disguised its severity, for the greatness of his language, his ability to rework tired old platitudes and make them sparkle anew but, most of all, for his wit, his incomparable aphorisms, his parables and paradoxes, in Ellman's estimation, 'so generous, so amusing and so right'.

We turn now to that other Portoran, Samuel Beckett, who inhabits a very different literary landscape to that of Oscar Wilde.

> who may tell the tale
> of the old man?
> weigh absence in a scale?
> mete want with span?
> the sum assess
> of the world's woes?
> nothingness
> in words enclose?

In this poem from the Addenda to the novel *Watt* (1953), written in France during the Second World War, Beckett forecasts his artistic intentions. Henceforth, his art will speak of old age; a time when decline, loss and solitude are to the fore. The contrast is between the young and the mature Beckett, between the facile and luxuriant language of the early works and the spare style of the later period. Between the artist who, albeit reluctantly, endorses the world, and the artist who rejects it.

Thus Beckett forged his artistic identity but the portents were present almost from the outset. Certainly, pessimism, the doctrine that evil preponderates over good and the sum total of human existence is, as a consequence, suffering and pain, is a factor in the early critical work *Proust* (1931). Drawing extensively on the arguments of the philosopher Schopenhauer, Beckett evokes a graphic metaphor – the Myth of Tantalus – to dramatise the black paradox at the heart of the human condition: that life is a constant striving for a satisfaction never achieved. We are, Beckett states in *Proust*, 'in the position of Tantalus with this difference, that we allow ourselves to be tantalised, and possibly the *perpetuum mobile* of our disillusions is subject to more variety'.

The second image Beckett borrows from Schopenhauer, and quotes approvingly in *Proust*, is contained in Calderon's dictum: 'For man's greatest offence / Is that he has been born'. Just as the Tantalus image affords an apt description of the misery of the human condition, then Calderon's line provides an apt explanation of its cause. 'Proust', argues Beckett, 'is completely detached from all moral considerations…Tragedy is the statement of an expiation, but not the miserable expiation of a codified breach of a local arrangement, organised by the knaves for the fools. The tragic figure represents the expiation of original sin, of the original sin of him and all his *socii malorum*, the sin of having been born'.

Similarly, the poems from the *Echo's Bones* (1935) collection, the short stories *More Pricks than Kicks* (1934), Beckett's first novel *Dream of Fair to Middling Women* (written in 1932 but only recently published), and the novel *Murphy* (1938) are replete with themes which preoccupy Beckett's mature fiction: the pessimism already mentioned, his fascination with the philosophical mind/body problem and the ascetic quest for nothingness and silence articulated in the poem from *Watt*.

Shortly after the war, Beckett returned to Ireland, dissatisfied and disillusioned with his work. Writing *Watt* had enabled him to clarify his literary preoccupations but the way ahead was far from clear. One night in March, he found himself at the end of Dun Laoghaire pier buffeted by a storm, when a vision or revelation occurred, which was to change his literary life and result in the kind of writing that has come to be defined as 'Beckettian'.

The revelation had two distinct aspects. Firstly, he would not struggle against the autobiographical nature of his writing, 'the dark he had struggled to keep under'; hereafter, all his writing would begin from within himself, with his memories and dreams, no matter how ugly and painful. Secondly, he would adopt the monologue form to tell these tales: no distancing was necessary between the teller and the tale. The incident is recalled with ironic overtones in the play, *Krapp's Last Tape* (1959); characteristically, Beckett did not exempt himself from satire.

Following his recognition of the direction his writing should take, Beckett returned to Paris and began writing again – in French. The next few years were the most productive of his literary career, although publishers for his work were hard to find. In this period, he wrote the trilogy of novels on which his reputation may ultimately rest, *Molloy* (1954), *Malone Dies* (1956) and *The Unnamable* (1958). He completed another novel, *Mercier and Camier* (1974) and several short stories.

At some point, when he was writing the trilogy, he turned to drama and 'began to write Godot as a relaxation, to get away from the awful prose I was writing at the time, [and] from the wildness and ruthlessness of the novels'. Thus *Waiting for Godot* (1954) the play which was to wrest him from the long obscurity he had endured as a writer sprang 'full blown' from Beckett's head in a very brief time. *Waiting for Godot* marked a significant upheaval in modern drama; the early productions were greeted with critical acclaim and also bafflement. The bleakness of the set, the strangeness of the protagonists, the black humour, all combined to create a work of tantalising ambiguity which paved the way for other experimental writers – Ionesco, Adamov and Pinter.

His later brilliant work, in the theatre and in prose narratives, is characterised by the quest for silence. Articulated in the earlier work, actively pursued in *Watt* and the trilogy, it became an obsession in the austere later period, as words aspire to but never quite reach the condition of silence. As he stated in *Worstword Ho*, 'Nothing else ever. Ever tried. Ever failed. No matter. Try again. Fail again. Fail better'. But omniscience and omnipotence as an artist, were never part of Beckett's plan. 'I am working with impotence, ignorance,' he once remarked in a rare interview. 'I don't think impotence has been exploited in the past. There seems to be an aesthetic maxim that expression is achievement – must be an achievement. My little exploration is that whole zone of being that has always been set aside by artists as something unusable – as something by definition incompatible with art.'

The Beckettian world is thus peopled by enfeebled, debilitated characters who endure an intolerable and austere existence, their anguished figures moving about a nullified Irish landscape. Yet far from being the unrelieved corpus of despair one might expect, Beckett's fiction is actually extremely humorous, the net result of his pessimism being, in the words of one commentator, 'a really entertaining complaint about life'. In the main, Beckett's humour relies on his treatment of the grotesque and the macabre. Witness Murphy, who burns to death in his garret, and has his last wish, that his remains be flushed down a toilet bowl in the Abbey Theatre, denied him. Instead the cremated ashes are scattered over the floor of a pub in the course of a drunken brawl.

Samuel Beckett, the boy who spent the years 1920 to 1923 in this Fermanagh of lake waters, islands and plains, was awarded the Nobel Prize for Literature in 1969 for 'a body of work that, in new forms of fiction and the theatre, has transmuted the destitution of modern man into his exaltation'.

We leave Enniskillen now, but not before mentioning 'The Bard of Knockmore', Peter Magennis, who wrote a novel *The Ribbon Informer* (1874), a volume of poetry and many other unpublished works. The well-known Ulster journalist, R. A. Wilson, who is better remembered by his pseudonym of *Barney Maglone*, lived and worked in Enniskillen over a century ago. An eccentric character, he wrote in a humorous dialect which was very popular all over the province of Ulster. And, in more recent times, Paddy Tunney, one of Ireland's best-known traditional singers and story-tellers, has produced two volumes of his autobiographical trilogy, *The Stone Fiddle* (1979) and *Where Songs do Thunder* (1991); a rich mixture of songs, legends, and stories of people and loved places, they convey a vivid picture of traditional life in rural Ireland.

Our destination is the Clogher valley, birthplace of William Carleton, whom Yeats described as 'the greatest novelist of Ireland by right of the most Celtic eyes that ever gazed from under the brow of a storyteller'. In his own words, he was 'born on Shrove Tuesday, the 20th of February, 1794, in the townland of Prillisk, in the Parish of Clogher, County Tyrone'. A few stones overgrown with grass are all that remain today of Carleton's birthplace but the house at Springtown, where he spent the impressionable years of his childhood, still stands. Carleton records, in his unfinished autobiography, how he idled away the fine summer evenings listening to the blackbirds singing in the beautiful hazel glen behind the house. Not far away is Kilrudden crossroads, where Ned McKeown and his wife Nancy lived, and it is there, in Ned McKeown's house, that Carleton's greatest work *Traits and Stories of the Irish Peasantry* (1830) begins. And just below Clogher is the stream called the Karry which Carleton leaped for a dare; a prodigious feat which resulted in the place being known ever after as 'Carleton's Leap'.

As well as having, what he termed, 'a good deal…of natural poetry in me', young Carleton received an education from the hedge schoolmasters of the time. Learned men, who knew Greek, Latin, Irish and English, as well as mathematics, they imparted their wisdom and love of knowledge to the young scholar, as well as the desire to succeed. First he toyed with the idea of a life devoted to the priesthood, but gave that aspiration up early and went to Dublin, where he began to write. In 1830, his collection of tales, *Traits and Stories of the Irish Peasantry* was published. A second volume appeared in 1833, and encouraged by the reception his stories had received, Carleton turned to the novel form. One of these, *The Black Prophet* (1847) recounts in painful detail the sufferings of the peasants in the Great Famine. Writing his autobiography was his last major task, but he died in January, 1869, leaving it unfinished.

Throbbing with life and vitality, Carleton's tales record faithfully a broken and complicated culture. A born storyteller, wildly funny and, yet, in the next instant, capable of a bleak and searing pathos. 'Any one at all acquainted with Ireland', he explained in the introduction to *Traits and Stories*, 'knows that in no country is mirth lighter, or sorrow deeper, or the smile and the tear seen more frequently on the face at the same moment'. 'Doesn't he become the pock-marks well, the crathur?' the parents of Phelim O'Toole say proudly of their hapless son, just recovered from smallpox. 'Become!' said the father; 'but doesn't the droop in his eye set him off all to pieces!' This extract also serves well to illustrate another of Carleton's achievements, namely, his ability to reproduce authentic dialect. As Thomas Flanagan notes in *The Irish Novelists 1800-1850* (1959): 'Half a century before John Synge put his ear to a Wicklow floor to catch the talk of servant girls, Carleton had caught every turn and nuance of Irish speech'.

And pervading all, his deep love for the landscape of the Clogher Valley. Expressed in simple terms in this description of one of his childhood homes: 'Nurchasy to me was paradise. The view from it of Fardress Glen, so beautifully wooded, and of Fardress grazing-fields, so green and extensive, together with the effect of these small circular groves, peculiar to some portions of the north, absolutely enchanted me. Nothing, in fact, could surpass my happiness. I frequently dreamt of the scenery about me, although I had it before my eyes every day in the week'. Or, woven into the atmospheric tapestry of his depiction of Christmas in Tyrone, and the torch-lit midnight mass, performed under the open sky, on the little mount behind the chapel: 'The scenery about the place was wild and striking; and the stars, scattered thinly over the heavens, twinkled with a faint religious light, that blended well with the solemnity of this extraordinary worship, and rendered the rugged nature of the abrupt cliffs and precipices, together with the still outline of the stern mountains, sufficiently visible to add to the wildness and singularity of the ceremony'.

In the churchyard of the present day Forth Chapel, which occupies the same site spoken of by Carleton in the quotation above, lies the grave of another Tyrone writer, the poetess Rose Kavanagh, who was buried there in 1891. A friend of the novelist Charles Kickham, Rose was born at Killadroy, near Beragh, Co Tyrone in 1859. When she was quite young, the family moved to Mullaghmore, beside the River Blackwater, in the parish of Clogher. Nearby, about two and a half miles north of Clogher and about one mile from Augher, lies the historic mill and beauty spot of Knockmany, the inspiring force, together with the River Blackwater, of a great deal of Rose Kavanagh's poetry. Although she established a niche for herself in the newspaper world in Dublin, and became quite involved in the political ferment of the time, her best poetry, characterised by an exquisite delicacy of expression, speaks of Tyrone: of Knockmany, 'whose proud face looks tenderly down on the plain', and the River Blackwater, 'fed with a thousand invisible rills, / Girdled around with the awe of the hills'.

By a rather circuitous route, we leave the Clogher Valley, and proceed to Sixmilecross, where the 'Bard of Tyrone', the Rev. W. F. Marshall, spent his childhood and the early years of his ministry. His father, Charles, was headmaster of Sixmilecross national school, and an entry, in copperplate handwriting, on 3 June 1895, denotes the day when he enrolled his two sons, William Forbes and Robert Lyons, as pupils in his school. The old school, situated about half-way down the main street of Sixmilecross still stands, but is no longer used for its original purpose. Nevertheless, it is not hard to envisage the young Marshall boys climbing the stone steps into the two-roomed school, and with their friends toeing 'a chalk line drawn / Upon a schoolroom floor'. Marshall and his place and his time are all summed up for me in an image given in a typewritten, and unsigned, description I found in Omagh library. In it W. F. and his friend 'Barelegged Joe', are seen racing down Strand Brae *en route* to Soshy's Pool to pit their wits against the 'Big Trout', the latter finally succumbing to Joe and his fiddle-string lasso.

Other local landmarks are immortalised in Marshall's verse. The title of the most recently published collection *Livin' in Drumlister* (1983) comes from Marshall's best known ballad, 'Me an' Me Da', which has been recited on concert platforms in locations as diverse as rural church halls and the National Theatre on London's South Bank. And, although W. F.'s poetic output was at its greatest when he lived and ministered in Castlerock, where 'the great seas roar / Along a Northern strand', it was his native hills and valleys that he yearned for:

But I was born in old Tyrone
And love the quiet things,
The burn that chucklcs round a stone,
The song a blackbird sings.

For Drumlister, Drumnakilly, Bernish Glen where the 'wee folk' skipped, but regrettably 'fairy ring / And elf-shot cow / And pixie king / Are fool talk now'; for Remackin River 'where the slender willows sway'; for Athenree and Shane Mill, where the green glen 'runs along to a little bridge of stone, / and the grey house stands beside a mill'; and 'the whins are covered with the gold of May again / and the whitethorn blossom has begun'. And above all, for Tullyneill, that 'green hill in Dark Tyrone'. In this, his most poignant and nostalgic poem, the dying poet recalls the Gaelic past of Tullyneill, (the hill of the O'Neills), and his own Plantation heritage; the schoolhouse where his father taught; the 'plain old house of God', where he had ministered; and the churchyard which would be his final resting place:

So maybe on another day
Lonesome I shall not feel
When I come back again to stay
Content in Tullyneill.

But Marshall also loved the people and language of Tyrone, and the characters he created are, perhaps, his greatest achievement. The frustrated bachelor contemplating marriage is a frequent theme. For example, from 'Me an' me Da',

I'm livin' in Drumlister,
An' I'm gettin' very oul',
I have to wear an Indian bag
To save me from the coul.

Or again, from 'Sarah Ann',

I'll change me way of goin', for me head is gettin' grey,
I'm tormented washin' dishes, an' makin' dhraps o' tay;
The kitchen's like a midden, an' the parlour's like a sty
There's half a fut of clabber on the street outby:
I'll go down agane the morra on me kailey to the Cross
For I'll hif to get a wumman, or the place'll go to loss…

Other, equally memorable, characters include Congo Maguire, the accomplished liar; the 'dhrunken scutcher's' son; or Our Son, just returned from America, whose wife is from Clare – 'she was raired in soot / An' she scrubbed a Yankee floor, / But now she's nothing from head to foot / But a jinglin' jooilry store'. All in all, a body of folk poetry which delightfully and humorously records a place, a language and a way of life that have all but disappeared.

Homeward bound, we travel through wild and deserted moorland to Pomeroy, Tyrone's highest village, and onwards through Cookstown towards Draperstown, where the Ballinascreen Historical Society have actively ensured that the local history and literature of this part of County Londonderry are recorded for posterity. Their publications include *The Wee Black Tin* (1980) which features poems by George Barnett and John Paul Kelly; Nora Ní Chatháin's poems under the title *The Heart of Ballinascreen* (1988); *The Poems of Geordie Barnett* (1991) in which 'the real mountainy man' gives poetic voice to his life-long infatuation with the landscape of the Sperrin Mountains; *Geordie Barnett's Gortin* (1992) and *In Crockmore's Shade* (1991) where John Paul Kelly, in simple, unpretentious word pictures portrays the joys and also the hardships of rural life in the first half of the twentieth century. And this rural writer's sense of place takes many forms; from the serenity of his tribute to 'The Sixtowns – One evening by the setting sun, / Moyard was in my view, / The lovely glade of mist and haze, / O'er Altayesky too,' to the harsh reality of 'March Winds' and his contention that 'Only those that dwell thereon, / A hillside farm in Ireland's ring, / Could know the list of hungry wants, / That circle round a scanty spring'.

Backtracking slightly, our arrival in Castledawson coincides with a return to the late twentieth century, and the zany life-style of the eccentric Gordon family, as recounted in Anne Dunlop's deliciously titled first novel, *The Pineapple Tart* (1992). From the opening moments of the novel, when a tea-bag is unceremoniously retrieved from the bin and washed under the tap to provide tea for the Reverend Adam Robinson, the narrator, Helen Gordon (the 'pineapple tart' of the title) records, in inimitable style, the vagaries of a wild but essentially innocent girlhood. One delightful episode finds Helen and her sisters taking part in a quaint local custom, peculiar to the seaside resort of Portstewart:

> Parading the Promenade on Sunday night is part of the mating ritual of all Presbyterians, and as Sarah was the only daughter to have what Mummy optimistically termed a 'marrying job' relationship we were dispatched to walk up and down the Prom with the intention of attracting the attention of some nice suitable young men. The nice suitable young men sat in cars along the double lines to disguise the fact that they had short legs, fat bums and red shoes.

We are quite close here to the traditional linen manufacturing district of Upperlands and should note that Wallace Clarke, who lives there, has written two books to do with sailing, one being an account of his experience of sailing around Ireland. His son Miles Clarke, has written a fine book about the life of his godfather, Miles Smeaton. Titled *High Endeavours*, it was published in Canada in 1991 and in England in 1993.

As the crow flies, it is only a few miles from here to the place where Seamus Heaney was born – where as a boy he watched the River Moyola 'pleasuring beneath alder trees', or paced the 'soft gradient' of Anahorish, his 'place of clear water'. However, today we must leave the rural splendours of Mossbawn, and like the young Seamus Heaney before us, follow the road to Derry city. It takes us to the west, over the spectacular mountain road via the Glenshane Pass, and down to Dungiven. Shaped by volcanic fire and glacial ice, the Sperrins are very old and very beautiful. Peat bog and moorland, relieved by dark patches of forest plantation stretch, lonely and remote, as far as the eye can see. Soon the colours soften, the grass grows lusher and we enter Dungiven, a small market town attractively situated at the foot of Benbradagh, and at the meeting point of three rivers, the Roe, the Owenreagh, and the Owenbeg. Two miles north of Dungiven, at Camish on the Limavady Road, John Mitchel, the third son of a Presbyterian minister, was born in 1815. Originally intended for the ministry, Mitchel worked in Londonderry, before entering a solicitor's office in Newry. A meeting with Thomas Davis in 1842 fired him with zeal for the nationalist cause, and in 1843, shortly after qualifying as a lawyer, he joined the Repeal Association.

In 1845, he began writing for the *Nation*, but its political stance was not radical enough for Mitchel, and in 1848 he founded the *United Irishman*. His views were uncompromising. In the pages of his paper he called for an armed insurrection to achieve an Irish republic which would secure 'the land for the people'. Alarmed by the reaction to his writings, the government rushed a special Treason-Felony Bill through parliament, and on the evening of 13th May, 1848, John Mitchel was arrested. On Saturday, 27th May, he was convicted of treason, and sentenced to fourteen years' transportation. *The Jail Journal* (1854) is a record of his time in captivity – of his experiences in Bermuda, where the ship first docked; from there to South Africa where an uprising of the colonists prevented the convicts from landing, and eventually to Tasmania where Mitchel was reunited with his wife and children, and worked as a farmer until 1853 when he escaped to America.

Surprisingly, since Mitchel left the Dungiven area when he was four years old, his memories of the district remained vivid. In one of the best known passages of the *Jail Journal*, he speaks of the river Shannon in Van Dieman's Land in evocative terms: 'Well I know the voice of this eloquent river: it talks to me, and to the woods and the rocks, in the same tongue and dialect wherein the Roe discoursed to me as a child; in its crystalline gush my heart and brain are bathed; and I hear, in its plaintive chime, all the blended voices of history, of prophecy, and poesy, from the beginning. I delight in poets who delight in rivers'.

Other works of Mitchel's include *The Life and Times of Aodh O'Neill, Prince of Ulster* (1846) and *The Last Conquest of Ireland (Perhaps)* (1861) but *Jail Journal* secured his literary reputation. As Arthur Griffith noted in his preface to the book, 'In the political literature of Ireland it has no peer outside Swift. In the literature of the prison it has no equal'.

A prison of a different kind holds Ann McGlone, the heroine of Frances Molloy's tragicomic novel *No Mate for the Magpie* (1985). The prison is Ireland, which she reckons is in an advanced 'state of chassis'. A native of Dungiven, Frances Molloy employs striking colloquial idiom to plot the life-story of Ann up to the age of twenty-two, when she stands one winter's night on O'Connell Bridge and watches the River Liffey *(Anna Livia)* surging through the bridge on its way out of Ireland, and comes to the conclusion that she must 'do the same an' go to a place where life resembled life more than it did here'. A magnificent strain of sustained black humour permeates the novel as Ann relates her life as a Catholic, growing up in Northern Ireland in the fifties and sixties. Sentimental rationalisations arising from a confused perception of religion are a favourite target:

> A wheen of months after he [Father Curry] came te our parish some men burnt down the house of a bad woman an' she had to jump out the upstairs window te escape. When she was in hospital Father Curry went an' heard hir confession an' brought her back inte the church again. The day after she got out of hospital she shot hirsel'. They say it was because she had repented of hir evil ways an' that god forgiv' her (isn't god good?)

An extremely funny and moving story told with great freshness and candour.

For the last stage of our journey we take the road to Limavady, where Miss Jane Ross, in 1851, noted down the haunting melody, known all over the world as the 'Londonderry Air'. Here, in Newtown Limavady, as it was then named, we meet William Makepeace Thackeray, the author of *Vanity Fair* who, in 1842 journeyed round Ireland, and recorded his perceptions of the country in *The Irish Sketch Book* (1843). In Ballyclose Street in the town, the 'wayward traveller' entered an inn, one rough October day, and promptly fell in love with the girl who served him a beaker of ale. A long poem was written in her praise, of which the best known lines are:

> Beauty is not rare
> In the land of Paddy,
> Fair beyond compare
> Is Peg of Limavady.

Moving onwards in time, several writers ensure the continuing status of Limavady in literary circles. One such is Harry Barton, who has written prose and drama for children and for an adult audience, and whose work has been broadcast and published. His books include the intriguingly titled *Yours Till Ireland Explodes, Mr. Mooney* (1973). His work combines humour with keen political comment. Another writer from Limavady is Audrey Scales. She has published one volume of poetry, *The Ephemeral Isle* (1983). Hendy Foy has written for children on a regular basis and his work has been broadcast by the BBC for many years. Patrick Macrory is another writer with strong Limavady connections (his great-great-grandfather moved from near Cookstown to Ardmore, in Co Londonderry, in the mid-nineteenth century to establish a mill). Macrory is best known for his contribution to local government reform in Northern Ireland. In addition to his historical writings (among them an account of the siege of Derry and a book about his family history) he has published one novel, *Borderline* (1937). Set in Limavady and the nearby village of Beltaine, this work owes much to the author's knowledge of local society.

Rejoining Thackerey's route, we recall his observation that:

> From Newtown Limavady to Derry the traveller has many wild and noble prospects of Lough Foyle and the plains and mountains around it, and of scenes which may possibly in this country be still more agreeable to him – of smiling cultivation, and comfortable, well built villages, such as are only too rare in Ireland.

Ballykelly and Muff (now Eglinton) are the villages Thackeray refers to, and he journeys through them, with a diversion by way of the Agricultural Seminary of Templemoyle, to Derry. And thus we end, back where the Foyle washes up to the walled city and with this eminent literary figure's first impressions of the ancient settlement:

> We had seen the spire of the cathedral peering over the hills for four miles on our way; it stands, a stalwart and handsome building upon an eminence, round which the old-fashioned stout red houses of the town cluster, girt in with the ramparts and walls that kept out James's soldiers of old.

Biographical Notes On Contributors

Select Bibliography

Key to Photographs

Index

Biographical Notes on Contributors

Sam Burnside was born in mid-Co Antrim and now lives in Londonderry. He was educated at The New University of Ulster at Coleraine and Magee University College, Derry; he holds a primary degree in English literature and a research degree for work on analysing readers' response to poetry. He has taught in secondary, further, higher and adult education. He now works in adult and lifelong education but in 1992 took an extended leave of absence from his post to establish the Verbal Arts Centre. His poetry and short stories have been published and broadcast widely and have attracted a number of awards, including a Hennessy/Sunday Tribune Award of Poetry, a Bass Ireland Literature Award, an Allingham Award for Poetry and the first University of Ulster, McCrea Award for Literature.

Cahal Dallat was born in Ballycastle, north-Co Antrim and now lives in London where he works as a computer consultant. He was educated at Queen's University, Belfast, where he studied statistics and operational research. He has an intense interest in Ireland's literature, history, culture and politics, and has written and given talks and lectures on issues of contemporary interest. A poet in his own right, his work has been published in, among other places, *Trio 7* (Blackstaff Press), *The Times Literary Supplement* and *The Guardian.*

Diarmaid Ó Doibhlin is Senior Course Tutor in Irish at the University of Ulster. Born at the Loup in south-Co Derry he was educated at St Patrick's College, Armagh. He is a graduate of the National University of Ireland. Dr. Ó Doibhlin is married with six children and lives in Magherafelt, Co Derry.

Bridget O'Toole is a writer and teacher who lives with her husband and their two children in Inishowen, Co Donegal. She taught English and American literature at the University of Ulster for a number of years and has published studies of Anglo-Irish women writers and of the novelist, J.G. Farrell. She was educated at Oxford where she took her primary degree; she holds an MA and a Ph.D. from Warwick University.

Marion Ross was born in Londonderry, and educated at First Derry Primary School, Magee University College, Derry and at the University of Ulster at Coleraine. She holds a primary degree in English and Philosophy and a D.Phil for her thesis on the works of Beckett and Schopenhauer. She lives near Derry city, is married with three children and is an occasional lecturer at the University of Ulster.

Select Bibliography

Allingham, William, *Laurence Bloomfield in Ireland,* New York, 1864

Barrington, Margaret, *My Cousin Justin,* London, 1939

Beckett, Samuel, *The Beckett Trilogy,* London 1979

Bonner, Brian, *Our Inis Eoghan Heritage,* 1972

Bullock, Shan, *Thomas Andrews, Shipbuilder*, Dublin/London, 1912; *After Sixty Years,* London, 1931

Burnside, Sam, *The Cathedral,* Belfast, 1989; *Walking The Marches*, Galway, 1990; *Horses,* Donegal, 1993; 'No Temporising with the Foe; Literary Materials Relating to the Siege of Derry', *The Linenhall Review*, Vol 5, No 3, Autumn 1988, pp 4-9 (Contains a discussion of the material, together with an extensive bibliography)

Carleton, William, *Traits and Stories of the Irish Peasantry*, New York, 1862; *The Black Prophet,* London, 1847

Cary, Joyce, *Castle Corner,* London,1938; *Mister Johnson,* Harmondsworth, 1939; *A House of Children,* London, 1941; *The Horse's Mouth,* London, 1944; *A Fearful Joy,* London, 1949

Colgan, John, *The Acta Sanctorum Hiberniae of John Colgan,* with an introduction by Brendan Jennings, Dublin, 1948 (A copy of John Colgan's *Acta Sanctorum Hiberniae* has been presented to, and is held by, the Inishowen Folk Museum, Bridge Street Carndonagh); *Trias Thaumaturga,* Louvain,1647

Coyle, Kathleen, *A Magical Realm,* New York, 1943

Deane, Seamus, *Celtic Revivals - Essays in Modern Irish Literature,* London, 1985; *A Short History of Irish Literature,* London, 1986; *Selected Poems,* Oldcastle, 1988; *The Field Day Anthology of Irish Writing,* Derry, 1991 (*The Field Day Anthology of Irish Writing* includes extracts from Heaney, Johnston, Cary, Friel, Macklin, Colgan, Sweeney, Toland, McGuinness and Deane)

Dunlop, Anne, *The Pineapple Tart,* Dublin, 1992; *The Soft Touch*, Dublin, 1993; *The Dolly Holiday*, Dublin, 1993

Farquhar, George, *The Beaux Stratagem,* London, 1976 (first staged 1707)

Fountain,The, The People of the Fountain, with Leon McAuley, Belfast/ Londonderry, 1993

Friel, Brian, *Three Sisters,* Dublin, 1981; *Selected Plays,* London, 1984; *Dancing at Lughnasa,* London, 1990; *The London Vertigo,* Oldcastle, 1990 (based on a play by Macklin)

Gebler, Carlo, *August in July*, London, 1986; *The Glass Curtain*, London, *1991*

Greacen, Robert, *A Garland for Captain Fox,* Dublin, 1975

Heaney, Seamus, *Sweeney Astray,* Derry, 1983; *Station Island*, London,1984; *New Selected Poems 1966-1987*, London, 1990; *Seeing Things,* London, 1991; *Preoccupations, Selected Prose 1968-1978,* London, 1980; *The Government of the Tongue*,London, 1988; *The Cure at Troy,* London, 1990

Johnston, Jennifer, *The Captains and the Kings,* London, 1972; *The Gates,* London 1973; *How Many Miles to Babylon?*, London, 1974; *Shadows on our Skin,* London, 1977

Kelly, John, *Grace Notes and Bad Thoughts*, Dublin, 1994

Kiely, Benedict, *Poor Scholar: a Study of the Days and Works of William Carleton,* London and New York, 1947; *A Journey to the Seven Streams: Seventeen Stories,* London, 1963; *Proxopera,* London, 1977

Macklin, Charles, *Four Comedies*, edited by J.O. Bartley, London, 1968 (The University of Ulster holds an edition of the plays at its Jordanstown campus)

Marshall, W.F., *Livin' in Drumlister*, Belfast, 1929

MacAnnaidh, Séamas, *Cuaifeach Mo Londubh Buí*, Dublin, 1983; *Mo Dhá Mhicí*, Dublin, 1986; *Rubble na Mickies*, Dublin, 1990; *Féirín, Scéalta agus Eile*, Dublin, 1992

McCafferty, Nell, *Peggy Deery,* London, 1989

MacGill, Patrick, *Children of the Dead End*, London, 1914; *Moleskin Joe,* London, 1923

McGlinchey, Charles, *The Last of the Name,* Belfast, 1986

McGuinness, Frank, *The Factory Girls*, 1982; *Observe the Sons of Ulster Marching towards the Somme,* London, 1986; *Innocence*, London, 1987; *Carthaginians* and *Baglady* , London, 1988

Milligan, Alice, *Poems*, edited with an introduction by Henry Mangan, Dublin, 1954

Molloy, Frances, *No Mate for the Magpie*, London, 1985

Montague, John, *Death of a Chieftain*, London, 1964; *The Rough Field*, Dublin, 1972

Ormsby, Frank, *A Northern Spring*, London, 1986

O'Brien, Flann [Brian O'Nolan], *At Swim-Two-Birds*, London, 1960; *The Dalkey Archive,* London, 1963; *An Béal Bocht*, Dublin, 1941. *The Third Policeman,* London, 1967

Ó Canáinn, Tomás, *Home to Derry*, Belfast, 1986

O'Donnell, Peadar, *Islanders*, London, 1928; *The Knife,* London, 1930

Ó Searcaigh, Cathal, *Suibhne: Rogha Dánta*, Dublin, 1988; *Homecoming / An bealach 'na bhaile; Selected Poems / Rogha Dánta,* Conamara, 1993

O'Sullivan, D.J., *From Fastnet to Inishtrahull*, Belfast, 1993

Sigerson, George, *Bards of the Gael and Gall,* London, 1897

Simmons, James, *Judy Garland and the Cold War,* Belfast, 1976; *Poems,* Dublin and Newcastle Upon Tyne, 1986

Sweeney, Matthew, *A Dream of Maps*, Dublin, 1981; *A Round House*, London,1983; *Blue Shoes*, London, 1989

Thackeray, William Makepeace, *The Irish Sketchbook*, 1843

Toland, John, *Christianity not Mysterious*, 1696

Wilde, Oscar, *Complete Works of Oscar Wilde,* London, 1948

Index

Key to Photographs

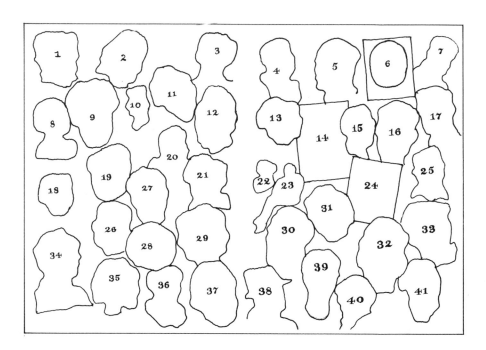

1	Kathleen Ferguson	22	Angela Doherty
2	Jennifer Johnston	23	William Carleton
3	Seamus Deane	24	Columcille (St. Columba)
4	Cecil Frances Alexander	25	Robin Glendinning
5	Robert Lloyd Praeger	26	Seamus Mac Annaidh
6	Col. John Mitchelburne	27	James Simmons
7	Patrick MacGill	28	John Mitchel
8	Margaret Barrington	29	George Farquhar
9	Seamus Heaney	30	Rose Kavanagh
10	Carlo Gebler	31	Kathleen Coyle
11	John Kelly	32	Samuel Beckett
12	Francis Harvey	33	Cathal Ó Searcaigh
13	George Berkeley	34	Joyce Cary
14	Farquhar play stage set	35	Frances Molloy
15	Peadar O'Donnell	36	Alice Milligan
16	Robert Greacen	37	Walter Hegarty
17	Shan Bullock	38	Flann O'Brien
18	Anne Dunlop	39	Benedict Kiely
19	Frank McGuinness	40	William Allingham
20	Patrick Macrory	41	George Sigerson
21	Frank Ormsby		

		DATE DUE